MAP

Art Center College

Peter Zec designing success

Peter Zec

designing success

Strategies
Concepts
Processes

Design Zentrum
Nordrhein Westfalen
Edition

Deutsche Bibliothek – CIP-Einheitsaufnahme
designing success / Peter Zec
Translated from the German by Keith Lunn
Original title: Mit Design auf Erfolgskurs
Cologne: DuMont, 1999

© 1999 Design Zentrum Nordrhein Westfalen Edition, Essen
First edition
ISBN 3-929 227-43-6

Editor: Jana Althöfer
Design: Christof Gassner
Production: Centrale Produktion Ingenfeld GmbH, Düsseldorf
Reproduction: Reprostudio S, Ljubljana
Printing: DELO tiskarna, Ljubljana
Printed in Slovenia

For Jana

The starting point for this book was an exhibition which I developed and presented together with Jana Althöfer as part of the Design Initiative of German Businesses in 1997. It was a kind of "design course", arranged as a travelling exhibition, which we gave the same title as this book. I received the commission for the exhibition project, which has in the meantime been shown at over ten different venues in Germany, from the German Association of Chambers of Industry and Commerce (DIHT), for which I should like to thank Dr. Kaiser once again most sincerely here. He it was who not only gave me the idea for the exhibition, but also arranged for the necessary funds.

The idea for this book, in turn, arose when I learned what a great response the exhibition of the same name was receiving from its numerous visitors. On the very first day of the presentation at the Tendence trade fair in Frankfurt am Main, large numbers of people spent time in the exhibition and in some cases took out their pads and pens to note down the accompanying texts. Many of the visitors even contacted me personally later to express their enthusiasm, often enquiring as to the availability of printed documentation.

Finally, I decided to take up the topic of the exhibition once again and rework it into this publication. There are of course evident parallels between the exhibition and the book, although the book provides an opportunity to present certain aspects in somewhat greater detail. Nevertheless, I aimed right from the start to express myself as concisely as possible in this publication too, as the great success of the exhibition was founded on just such concision.

Neither the exhibition nor, and much less, this book, could have ever come into being without the support of the numerous companies which appear there. I should like to express my gratitude to all of them once again here. Furthermore, I should like to thank Thomas Hauffe, who made publication of this book by the Dumont-Verlag possible in what is a very short time for publishing houses. Further thanks are due to Christof Gassner, whose design makes a major contribution to the better understanding of this book.

Finally, my special thanks go to Jana Althöfer, who assisted me with great commitment both in the presentation of the exhibition and in my work on this book. In doing so, she remained an understanding and loving companion at all times. I should like to dedicate this book to her in the hope of many more joint projects.

Peter Zec
Essen, July 1998

Intro

Keeping a business going is by no means such an easy job in today's world. Many companies, some long established, have in the past had to face up to the fact that they were no longer able to keep pace with the demands placed on products and sales arguments, leading all too often to their disappearance. Other companies which once bore great, resounding names, have only just managed to survive under different names as subsidiaries of a stronger competitor or investor.

Small and medium sized enterprises above all are affected particularly seriously by the ever fiercer and inexorable competition on the extensively globalised markets of the western business world. Many of these enterprises were, up to now, used to selling products of sound quality successfully at a reasonable price, without having to think of any further-reaching development and marketing strategies at all. These good times, as we have known for a while now, are past.

Instead, businesses today are confronted with completely new challenges. With the opening of the eastern European countries' borders to the west and the flow of new, cheap goods onto the lucrative markets of western nations, many manufacturers are faced at a stroke with the necessity to rethink and reorientate themselves towards other competitive advantages if they are to secure their own survival. One of these strengths is doubtless design!

Today, design is an important topic in particular for those enterprises which no longer rely on quantity-orientated action, but instead and increasingly on qualitative success factors. For only in this way will it be possible in the long term to escape ruinous price competition with manufacturers from Eastern Europe or South East Asia. With design, these businesses can embark on a new course to success.

For many companies, being successful first means being able to survive. A course to success therefore in some way describes a path to survival which enterprises can follow to secure their existence. There is certainly not just one path leading to this goal. On the contrary, it is highly conceivable that there may be easier or harder, or even parallel ways.

If, then, this book describes a course to success by design, this does not mean that there are no other opportunities and alternatives. But the path via design is a path on which one can orientate oneself very well by following the examples of other businesses which have successfully followed this route for a long time. Orientation in this case can also mean that others can give one the courage to do as they do. For courage and an unconditional will to succeed are now more than ever before the most important conditions for taking a new departure and ensuring the survival of an enterprise.

Many entrepreneurs and managers nowadays appear incapable of or unwilling to display that courage. Instead, they stick to well trodden paths that lead nowhere, and are probably hoping for a miracle to save them from destruction.

A strategy which places design at the centre of entrepreneurial activity is more promising, as evidenced by many businesses in almost all sectors of industry. Some of them, and their specific approaches, are presented in this book.

It must be remembered in this context that although the businesses mentioned as examples here are each presented against a particular thematic background, this does not mean that they are only exemplary and successful in that regard. Most of these companies have in the meantime managed to set their own, high standards in almost all areas where design is applied.

This book is addressed to all those who wish to give their businesses and their daily entrepreneurial activities a higher quality through design. The numerous examples, explanations and recommendations in this book will provide them with a thorough introduction to the various applications of design. The individual focal topics have been selected and presented in such a way that it is also, and above all, possible for those not so familiar with design issues to gain their initial bearings, to recognise opportunities and potential applications, and to understand the growing importance of design.

The book is not intended to be a textbook, but rather a book to learn from, and one which at the same time aims to be enjoyable and motivate its readers to take a first step into the world of design. The directions and length of the "course to success" described here are consciously selected to allow the destination to be reached with interest in the subject but without any major effort – a destination which can however only be a temporary one, because in the ideal case it represents a starting point for the reader's own design-orientated actions.

For the sake of better understanding, I have refrained from over-complex and extensive descriptions. The straightening out of certain passages to simplify matters is, I think, fully justified, as design today is no longer something exclusively for the experts, but rather a future-related task for all decision-makers in businesses and for specialists in marketing, sales and trade, in corporate communications and for management consultants. This book can be of use to all of them. Not to purvey a new truth, or to be right where others are wrong, but to put them on the course – should they wish to accompany me along this road – to designing success!

1

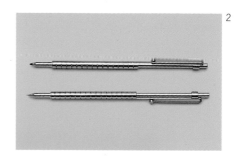

2

3

"Design is the sum total of all efforts aimed at making industrial products not only technically functional, but also tastefully and artistically perfect. In that context, good form is not just a fashionable wrapping. Apart from their utility value, designed products mostly confer additional benefits and have a sales-promoting effect."

Gabler Wirtschaftslexikon

"In our work and leisure, we are surrounded at every instant by a multitude of things which have been manufactured industrially, in series, and with more or less taste: from the watches on our wrists to ballpoint pens, from spectacles to scissors, from cars to jet planes. In the household with its various electrical appliances, in the office with word processors and calculators, in sports with skis and golf clubs, etc., or in the armed forces with their weapons, rockets and battleships – we are constantly confronted by countless products whose basis is always a forward-looking instant, a creative drawing, a draft to give them shape, and which are derived from the circumstance of duplicating, mechanical mass production. These are products which belong to mankind's environment and influence mankind."

Gillo Dorfles (1964)

4

7

5

6

1 With the chronograph – ref. no. 5360.28 – the Swiss watch manufacturer M & M presents a unique new design line in the chronometer field. The design is by Georg Plum-Plum Design.

2 LAMY spirit ballpoint and propelling pencil in a new form. Design: Wolfgang Fabian

3 Frame R 2478. Optische Werke G. Rodenstock. Design: Peter Kovari

4 Aircraft can also be design objects.

5 Plak Control Ultra OL 9545 dental hygiene set. Braun AG is well known for good design in various product categories.

6 Chief designer Bruno Sacco produced a real design innovation with the SLK Roadster of Daimler Chrysler AG.

7 IBM Think Pad 560. Weighing 1.9 kilograms and 31 millimetres thick, this notebook is a slim, lightweight companion. It communicates with printers and other computers via an infrared interface, dispensing with cables. Design: Richard Sapper In-house design: Hisashi Shima and Kazuhiko Yamazaki

Introduction

13

1

2

What design is not!

Design is not art!
Design is also not art making itself useful!

"Art produces originals, design series.
Art is there for its own sake.
Design is a contract-related service.
Design needs considerable objectivity.
Art is subjective.
Design enters into intelligent compromises.
Art excludes them.
Design is orientated towards the feasible.
Art towards utopia.
Design must be comprehensible.
Art does not have to be.
Design proceeds from established customs.
Art leaves them behind."
    Kurt Weidemann

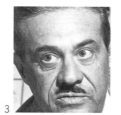

1 Pablo Picasso contributed many interesting works of art to our lives. But design was never his field.

2 Andy Warhol broke through established ways of thinking and seeing in his work. His art has provided much inspiration for design. Warhol started his career as a designer, but only achieved international fame as an artist.

3 Raymond Loewy ranks among the most successful designers of the 20th century. Many of his product designs helped the clients to save costs and beat their competitors on the market.

4 Hans Gugelot is one of the great pioneers of post-war German design. His product designs established a worldwide reputation for Braun.

  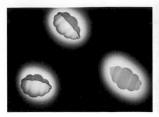

1

2

Pasta (alimentary paste) is simply a starchy food preparation made from semolina, and can take on an almost infinite variety of shapes. Ribbons, cords, tubes … there are no limits to the imagination. The special thing about it is that the form of a particular type of pasta determines its taste, although as a rule the same ingredients have been used as for all the others.

With cars, design is decisive. The fascination of an automobile is to a great extent the fascination of form.

If we are honest, rationality plays only a subordinate role in car buying decisions. There are hardly any major differences to be found between the technical specifications of models in the various classes, and prices have also moved very much into line. When a budget has been determined, the decision to purchase is predominantly guided by emotional factors, feelings and taste.

3

4

1 The design of the Renault Twingo made the world go crazy. The Renault designers demonstrated their courage and were successful. In France, the Twingo is still the number one selling petrol engined auto-mobile. In Europe, it ranks among the seven best selling cars.

2 The original design of the Nissan Micra was planned to last, and did. The model was restyled in 1998 to bring it back into line with the changing tastes of young people. A Nissan market analysis reveals that the Micra functions as an entry model bringing new customers to the brand. The Micra's design therefore makes a great contribution to market development.

3 The design of the Ford Ka is not only unusual, but also characteristic of a new understanding of form in design. The aim of the development was to produce a car that perfectly reflected the style of the present with no compromises. The result is a new automobile design which will have a decisive influence on the aesthetic taste of the future.

4 The A class from DaimlerChrysler combines a new philosophy of driving with a completely new design. The focus is on the optimisation of use. The comfortable sill height and the dimensions of the interior belie its classifi-cation as a small car. The design of the A class aims to reflect a new spirit of life. A car with an unmistakable character is the result.

Introduction

17

Product

devel

The development of new products has to fulfil various demands if those products are to be successful on today's extensively saturated markets. Above all, they have to possess one or preferably several characteristics which distinguish them from competing products. For only in that way is it possible to achieve a unique position for a product on the market and thus create a more favourable starting point for the sales success which is the aim. But this, as we have seen often enough in the past, is much simpler to express in theory than it is to implement in practice.

In numerous sectors of industry, the competing companies have now reached the limits of their capacity for technical innovation in product development, with the result that hardly any notable distinctions can now be made. Furthermore, cost factors are making an increasing number of businesses reluctant to enter into price competition. Only 26 percent of German manufacturers still aim to assert themselves on the market by offering lower prices. Independently of that, however, all the German manufacturers agree that higher quality is the most important basis for the success of their products.

The quality of a product can take many forms, and is determined by various factors. The decisive thing is, though, for the special quality of a product to be recognisable at first sight. Making this possible is as a rule the function of design. But design can only meet that demand when it is not misinterpreted as a kind of product cosmetics or styling, but instead plays an appropriate role right from the start in the product development process. Design has to be included in the development process as an integral product characteristic: as a kind of beauty emanating from the inside of the product and not merely a striking superficial gleam, but rather a credible and persuasive overall aesthetic impression. Where design is appropriately integrated in product development in this way, products can be given a characteristic appearance and image, truly setting them apart from the competition.

"The Braun Sixtant",
according to Hans
Wichmann, was "the
best designed and most
elegant mains powered
shaver of the sixties.….
In this appliance, Hans
Gugelot accentuated
the effect of black and
silver to constitute a
presentation value for
the first time. Those
colours were to be part
of the Braun corporate
identity from then
on. The effect, however,
does not come from
the colours alone, but
above all from the
haptically and optically
impressive surface
treatment: the brushing
makes the simple black
plastic and chromium
steel appear to be
precious materials."

Good form

The modern successor to the Braun Sixtant is the Flex Integral 6550, and Braun is still setting design standards today with this shaver. Over and above the "good form", the product has an additional emotional appeal which captures the spirit of the age.

"Good industrial form" (die gute Industrieform) was a result of an "honest" product design, freed from ornamentation and embellishment. The focus was on the perfection of function and utility by a simple, appropriate design for the purpose. The entrepreneurs Erwin and Artur Braun, who, inspired by designer Wilhelm Wagenfeld, started in 1954 to search for a new way of product development and business management, are a typical and ideal example of this approach. Their aim was to express more "honesty and humanity" in product design. This took place in the 50s and 60s, at a time when radios – as they thought – were simply crying out "to be freed from their bombastic golden phoniness".

Together with designer Hans Gugelot, the Braun brothers managed to establish a new design standard in product development internationally with their modern products. The Braun company has made history with its product design, and continues to do so, earning recognition worldwide. The striving for good form at Braun is consistently pursued as the idea of a new product culture which is not rigidly orientated towards a formal design principle, but rather aims at continuous optimisation of utility quality. That is why design is integrated in product development from the start. This will surely be one fundamental reason why Braun has also become the most commercially successful company in its industry with global market leadership in several product categories. Thanks to the good form of

Example
Braun AG, Kronberg

Product development

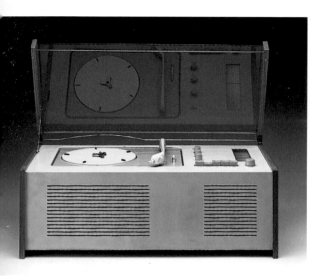

The "SK 4" radiogram, affectionately known as "Snow White's coffin", now ranks among the classics of "good form". An outstandingly successful product development that exerted a strong influence worldwide, not least on account of its Plexiglas cover. Design: Hans Gugelot and Dieter Rams, 1955/56

its products, the company has been able to achieve a continuous growth in sales and profits in recent years, despite the recession.

Ideally companies will succeed in meeting ethical and social aims as well as achieving the business aim of making a profit by orienting their products on the demands of good form. According to this way of looking at things it is not enough to be a success on the market with design unless it also improves the quality of our lives in society. Good product form is always accompanied by the development of better forms of living. This notion of good form is nowadays well established in German design. Good form is also the right form because it is born of functional necessity, perfected beyond its visual appearance by optimal utility of the product.

Proponents of good form nevertheless often adhere to rigid functionalistic design principles, which then lead to the creation of all too simple or very boring products which may at best impress the market with their technical function, but not with an interesting design.

Do not be afraid to incorporate appropriate variations in the product design without necessarily impairing the function and use of the product. The development of good form in Braun design from the 50s to the present day provides us with an excellent example of this.

Today's designers are also proud to create products for Braun. In an advertisement, frog-design studios publicise the "Thermoscan plus" ear thermometer designed for Braun AG. Source: Design Report magazine 1/98

Loewe systems.
The components are
reduced to the
necessary minimum.
Design: Phoenix
Produkt Design

Credo 7581 ZP.
The form symbolises
the power of innovation.
Design: Phoenix
Produkt Design

Innovations need design

Product innovations can arise in a variety of ways:

By increasing technical efficiency, using better materials, expanding the potential areas of use and many, many more. Most of these innovations can only be implemented by a new design of the product. It is however important for the newness of a product to be recognised and understood by prospective customers on the market. This is a typical function of design. The aim must be to give the innovative product a new, appropriate form.

**Example
Loewe Opta GmbH
Kronach**

The decisive factor, then, is a visual presentation of the innovative nature of a product. Loewe Opta GmbH has been doing this in an exemplary fashion for many years. With a systematic incorporation of design practised with remarkable continuity, the company has been able to underpin and even expand its market position as a home electronics premium brand.

In the early 80s, when many German home electronics businesses experienced a serious crisis caused by the innovation and price offensive of their Japanese competitors, the responsible managers at Loewe Opta had the courage to embark on a completely new course. While product development at most German television set manufacturers was lagging one to two years behind the new trends from Japanese competitors, Loewe Opta took the decision systematically to back the symbiosis of innovation and poignant design. Instead of entering into ruinous price competition with the Japanese manu-

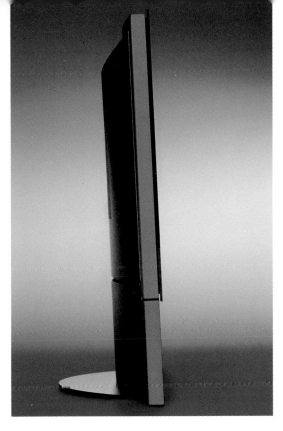

The prototype of the Loewe systems plasma screen uses the futuristic 16:9 format. The screen diagonal is 107 cm, and the casing depth a mere 14 cm. Innovation and design are the basis of the Loewe products' success.
Design: Phoenix Produkt Design

facturers, as the other German companies did, the Loewe managers relied on quality competition, with the result that the company has been extremely successful up to the present day with a continuous technical development of its products.

The early and systematic incorporation of design in product development is an absolutely essential factor in this success. With their original and authentic design, which points appropriately to technical perfection, Loewe products simultaneously stand out from the multitude of interchangeable mass produced articles and thus achieve a special market position.

This development was initiated with the "Loewe Art 1" TV set launched in 1985, heralding a new era in pedestal mounted televisions. Even then, the decisive factor behind its success was the new design. Today, the company also produces complete hi-fi systems, in which the design of the individual components is carefully blended into the overall aesthetic appearance of the group. Loewe Opta products have won numerous awards in the past for their high quality, innovative design.

Product development

Compact Performance
CPV pneumatic
valve block. Festo KG
has long followed
a systematic design
strategy.

A new language of form
was developed for the
entire product range.
Compact Performance
CPE single pneumatic
valve from Festo KG.

Example
Festo AG & Co.
Esslingen

The interaction between technical innovation and innovative design is however not only promising for manufacturers of consumer goods, but also allows better market opportunities to be achieved in the capital goods sector. Festo, for example, has pursued an exemplary design strategy in its product development for many years. The company manufactures, among other things, series of pneumatic valves which have to withstand the highest loads and satisfy the highest demands for precision. In order to express the special quality and innovative technology in a convincing manner at first sight, and thus also to strengthen clients' confidence in the company's expertise, a new language of form was developed for the pneumatic valve series and is to be applied to the entire Festo range. The company invests systematically in design because it clearly distinguishes itself from competitors in that way. Design creates confidence!

In many companies, design is still regarded as additional, unnecessary work which causes costs and does not pay. They rely on products selling on the basis of their technical characteristics or their representing value for money. This may still be promising in situations of demand, but not on markets which are characterised by saturation and superfluity.

Don't rely on your traditional strengths for too long!
Don't be afraid to innovate, in design too!
Take a leaf out of Festo's or Loewe Opta's book: both companies which followed that path uncompromisingly in difficult economic times and have remained successful up to the present day. Many major companies in the German home electronics industry and in other sectors could still be there today if they had acted courageously in time.

Tupperware "Swing
Boxes" are versatile
containers with
swing-like lids.

Design assures quality

Nowadays, products have to do more, cost less and fit into
existing worlds. The demands of today's customers have
reached a very high level, and the trend is still rising. More
quality, wherever possible at the same price, is the customers'
watchword. At the same time, more and more companies are
facing rising production costs and dwindling trading margins,
which makes it more and more difficult for them to improve or
even maintain the quality standards they once set.

In situations like this, design can make a very good contribution to assuring or improving quality. Often, namely, it is first
and foremost a question of design whether, for instance, a new,
equivalent quality can be produced with cheaper materials or
surface treatment methods. The decisive factor is not betraying
the trust of customers once it has been attained: a typical task
for design!

But how can design contribute to the creation or assurance
of a specific product quality? This depends on design being
pursued not as a kind of superficial product cosmetics, but in a
direct relationship with the use and functionality of a product.
Only in this way is it possible to confer a new quality on industrial products which goes beyond their purely technical and
material properties. What is meant here can be illustrated very
well by the success of the products from the Tupperware
company.

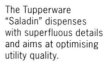

The Tupperware "Saladin" dispenses with superfluous details and aims at optimising utility quality.

Tupperware's "Young Wave" is notable for its robustness, transparency and the special tactile quality of the material surface.

Tupperware products are as a rule plastic products manufactured from polyethylene or polycarbonate. Most of the company's customers, however, will hardly be in a position to tell that these materials are not just simply plastic, but plastic of the highest quality. But even if the materials and manufacturing processes used satisfy demands for the best quality, it is nevertheless something else on which the extremely great success of Tupperware products and the high regard in which they are held are based: in contrast to numerous other products, it is the special form of use and the functionality which are recognised by most of the customers as features of special quality. This type of quality is at the same time the special quality of the design which unmistakably identifies Tupperware products.

Tupperware design does not follow any stylistic development, nor does it indicate its identity by any external frills: on the contrary, each individual product represents the perfection of a functional rationality taken shape. It is not the form itself that typifies Tupperware design, but the way in which it optimises the use of every single product. A characteristic feature is the strict avoidance of superfluous details and concentration on the essential elements of functional handling. In this way, one sees immediately that the special quality of these products arises from a striving for industrial perfection which does not contain even the smallest hint of handicraft or folklore. The design serves to put this claim to high quality into the right shape again and again, even when details are continually refined.

**Example
Tupperware GmbH
Frankfurt am Main**

Product development

Problem

More and more companies unthinkingly fall into the trap of a ruinous price war with their competitors, and in doing so they make it impossible for them to be successful with better quality.

Recommendation

For small and medium sized enterprises in particular, it is becoming more and more important to back quality rather than pure quantity. Quality arguments can achieve better distinctions in the long term than mass offers at a better price. Products should signal a high level of design quality starting with their external appearance.

Independently of the actual use of a product, however, design can also express quality in a different, almost symbolic way. This is made possible, for instance, by consciously applying a particular form of design to bring a product into the associative ambit of another product which is already regarded as a guarantee of quality. In the positive, legitimate case, this can lead to a kind of image or sympathy transfer from one product to another. In the negative, illegitimate case, though, manufacturers often shamelessly imitate products from their competitors, so as to profit from the others' success. I shall go into that in more detail elsewhere. Here, I should first like to consider a positive example of quality-orientated image transfer by design. That, namely, was convincingly achieved by the automobile manufacturer BMW with the development of the Z3.

Example
BMW AG, Munich

With the Z3, BMW created a new sports car that must have attracted envy from competitors across the globe, and not only because it became the successor to the legendary Aston Martin as the new, contemporary James Bond vehicle, but also because its specific design establishes a link with a great BMW tradition – one which only a few competitors have anything to compare with. Quite consciously, the BMW designers brought the design of the Z3 into an unmistakable aesthetic proximity to that of the also legendary BMW 507 from the fifties. The external similarity between the Z3 and the roadster which ranked as one of the most beautiful sports cars in the world thirty-five

In the Z3 roadster, the BMW design team consciously echoes the great tradition of the past, so as to emphasise the special quality of the model.

years earlier is certainly not a matter of chance. On the contrary, BMW is consciously establishing a design reference to the great tradition of former years, so as to express the special quality of the Z3 a priori. The huge success of the new product proves that the BMW managers have followed the right strategy.

Product development

In many industries now, products which are to be successfully marketed have to do more than just function well. They frequently have to have an additional implicit value, which is not to be confused with the creation of an additional technical and functional benefit. Nowadays, the decisive factor is for us to recognise a certain "higher" value in products. What could that be?

A glass which is merely good enough to drink out of may well not fulfil the demands of higher value. To do that, it would have to have a further special characteristic. It would, for example, have to be fun to give or receive as a gift. For a long time now cars, too, have not been acquired merely as useful means of transport, but also have to generate the driving pleasure the advertising promises.

As we entered a new age of information and communication, it became time to reflect upon a new, contemporary image of mankind in design, which has replaced the "homo faber" with his enthusiasm for technology. More and more people are guided more strongly in their actions by the emotional experience of things. This new type is a sensitive person with a penchant for the playful and adventurous; a kind of "homo ludens". Designing products for this type of person means emotionalising their language of form. Products of that kind must not only be functional, but also friendly and fun.

The creation of higher implicit value is now one of the most important functions of design in many sectors of industry. In

"2 Hands"
symbolises the ideal
image of a basket.
Authentics GmbH.
Design:
Konstantin Grcic

The "Rondo" shopping
bag.
Authentics GmbH
Design:
Hansjerg Maier-Aichen

"Cap" waste paper
basket. The design
gives a familiar every-
day object the
appearance of some-
thing unique.
Authentics GmbH.
Design:
Hansjerg Maier-Aichen

contrast to utility value and exchange value, the higher implicit value of a product cannot as a rule be recognised as an objective quantity.

Higher implicit value can, for instance, express itself as a subjective preference for an (aesthetic) detail. It has more to do with worlds of emotion than with common sense. After all, what we are dealing with is the personal world view of an autonomously acting sentient being.

This simultaneously signifies the end of product concepts based solely on the ideology of reason at the horizon of future product developments. Products nowadays no longer have to be perfect in all respects, but have to be capable of awaking desire and seducing.

It is the beauty of seduction in the positive sense which enters the game of design here. That this of course has to be played on a high level of quality and should go hand in hand with a striving for innovation requires no discussion.

Hansjerg Maier-Aichen with his company Authentics manages again and again to market bestsellers that possess the beauty of seduction in the form of a higher implicit value. He has coined the term "poetic everyday objects" for these. Higher implicit value stems from a design which aims to confer the form of something unique on normal, well-known everyday objects: a basket, a table lamp, a soap dispenser, and so on. "Reduction means more to us than disdainful omission. Pure omission

Example
Authentics artipresent
Holzgerlingen

Product development

33

Always upright, the
Sony RM-S78T remote
control takes a playful
look at television.
Sony Deutschland
GmbH

"Pinguin" razor
basta. Innovation &
Design GmbH
Design: Dirk Stange
Design

rapidly leads to pure boredom. Our reduction", the product
catalogue states, "is not unconditional simplification, but rather
a double process, in principle acting in opposite directions: the
increasingly precise polishing to produce additional beauty in
the form, the material, the light – and the consistent removal of
the superfluous." This contemporary reinterpretation of the less
is more principle is what finally leads to market success.

Design generates higher implicit value by providing products
with playful and emotional characteristics over and above their
functional qualities. One especially elegant example of this can
be found in the world of home electronics in the form of the
Sony RM-S78T remote control, which is designed as a pop-up
figure. Always upright, it takes a playful approach to television.

The "Pinguin" razor designed by Dirk Stange also has the
characteristics of a pop-up figure and promises more fun during
the daily shave. The special higher value of this everyday object
consists in the fact that it has a friendly appearance as an
object alone, which at times even surpasses its utility value as
a razor.

Products like the remote control from Sony or this razor
put more fun into the world of banal everyday products, and also
show that it is perfectly possible to take new departures in
product development, no matter whether in the high tech or low
tech fields.

Many product developers, above all engineers with their enthusiasm for technology, still tend to bring a maximum of perfection to their products. For them, a good solution has to stand on a firm foundation and be improved again and again. But this costs time and money. Products which meet this development target in all respects are often too late on the market and too expensive. An excessive fear of inappropriate wittiness and banality then also frequently robs these products of the necessary seductive power.

It is not always absolutely necessary to refine products to a maximum of perfection: that may well be absurd. It is more important to design them in such a way that they have an added value in terms of emotional appeal, which draws a kind of "wow" response from us. Interestingly, the price then plays a subordinate role with products of this kind. Their appeal does not as a rule result from their technical perfection, but from the emotional longing their design awakes in us. It goes without saying that these products nevertheless have to function perfectly on a technical level.

Corporate
commu

The interaction between design and communication is especially important wherever markets have reached a degree of saturation which brings about fierce competition. Under such conditions, it is no longer sufficient in many of today's industries to put perfectly manufactured and well designed products on the market at a reasonable price, but in addition it is more and more decisive for the special qualities and fine distinctions of a product to be made clearly visible in an appropriate setting. This is one of the fundamental tasks of communication!

By means of communication, it is possible to create a symbolic system of meaning and sense which forms the setting for the market appearance of a product. Successful businesses have long known that the form of communication is just as important for commercial success as the form of a product. This does not of course mean that good communication can compensate for bad design. However, it is indeed possible for well designed products to appear in an even better light with an appropriate form of communication. In this way, a significant increase in the attention of potential purchasers can be achieved.

But design also needs communication for a totally different reason: Because, namely, most of the customers are not exactly design experts themselves, there have to be communicative concessions if they are to recognise fine and advantageous (design) distinctions. Often, it is only these fine points which determine whether a product is purchased or not. The particularly difficult aspect of this situation is however that we are not dealing here with decisions based on objectifiable matters of fact, but with the predominantly subjective, individual motivation that leads a purchaser to prefer one product over another. It is therefore ideal when communication with the customer can take place on an emotional level. This is mostly the case when a company succeeds in creating a world in common with its products and its customers, in which the design of objects and situations in life are thought about and spoken about in similar ways. Communication is then to be understood as the mutual shaping and forming of a common world by joint action. For this to happen, businesses must recognise that they have to communicate with their potential customers in a suitable way. The manufacture of good products alone is by no means sufficient any longer.

Design shapes identity

What do companies like BMW, Deutsche Bank, IBM and Lufthansa have in common?

If you know these companies, you will recognise them everywhere. They all have a highly pronounced identity which ensures that they are unique and unmistakable. They have understood that it is important to have an easily recognisable image everywhere and all the time. They have therefore managed to be easily identifiable and thus themselves become brands.

A company's image is determined by several factors, such as what the business does, the quality it aims to achieve, the way in which it interacts with its customers, the way its employees behave, and the responsibility it takes on for the environment and society. All in all, the impression outside observers have of an enterprise is essentially created by the way it distinguishes itself from other businesses. But distinctions are always the result of decisions. People distinguish by deciding in favour of one thing and against another. The more determination behind a decision, the more clearly visible the distinction that results.

Businesses also distinguish themselves from one another by making decisions. By deciding to do one thing and not another, they set themselves apart from other enterprises. In the beginning, therefore, there is always the decision, which makes the difference, which in turn leads to the identity. Strength in decision making is thus an essential condition for a strong identity.

Many responsible managers do not have the courage to make independent and unequivocal decisions on the form of communication, the design of the products or the orientation towards a defined target. Instead, they follow the decisions they have observed at other companies and imitate these more or less precisely. This makes it very difficult, if not totally impossible, for many companies to develop a clearly recognisable identity of their own.

The development of a corporate identity demands courageous, clear decisions and the ability to rethink these systematically again and again. The starting point is self-recognition, which in turn leads to new decisions on functions, problems and objectives. In the course of this process, independent and unequivocal decisions have to be made on how to distinguish all the forms of the corporate image, ranging from the design of the product environment and products to the design of forms of communication with customers, staff and the public at large, from others.

Distinctions are always made in a certain form. This is why, and the only reason why, they can be recognised at all. In consequence, it is also the form of the distinction that determines the identity as unmistakable and unique.

The company: Rodenstock is a manufacturer of lenses and frames for spectacles, and various optical precision instruments. The company has a history spanning almost 100 years, with no dramatic caesuras. Many businesses would look back on such a history with a certain pride and be satisfied with the status quo, ensuring that everything remained as it was. For a number of years, however, things have been different at Rodenstock. Here, starting with a conscious process of self-discovery, the staff have embarked on new ways of corporate development with the aim of securing the company's existence in the long term. The starting point was the decision by corporate management to question what had gone before, so as to arrive at a clear basis for new decisions.

Self-recognition: In several workshops, managers and staff from various areas and departments in the company examined the question of Rodenstock's identity. They attempted to define it by observing the enterprise in the environment it had itself created, and tried to distinguish it from other businesses.

In this process, the staff recognised that Rodenstock had up to then presented itself and its products in a non-uniform, unco-

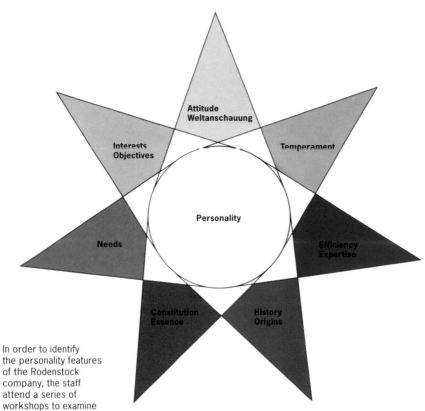

Attitude
Weltanschauung

Interests
Objectives

Temperament

Personality

Needs

Efficiency
Expertise

Constitution
Essence

History
Origins

In order to identify the personality features of the Rodenstock company, the staff attend a series of workshops to examine what characteristics, qualities and values the organisation has. The objective is to develop a personality model.

ordinated and contradictory scenario. As a result, and an unde-tected one up to then, the company had been unconsciously working against its own interests, which would presuppose the development of a strong, independent identity. Rodenstock should be clearly recognisable to all its customers, always and everywhere, with a well perceptible difference from competing companies. But that was not the case at the time, as the company's presentation was much too run of the mill and inter-changeable, and thus not clearly distinguishable, both in the form of its communications and in the design of the products. The success the company had enjoyed up to that time was therefore less attributable to its special identity than to other efforts, whose effectiveness would however be highly doubtful in future.

The task: Starting with the process of self-recognition, the decision was taken at Rodenstock to shape the company's iden-tity better than before with the aid of communications and design, so as to give it a higher, clearer profile and at the same time make it easier to distinguish. "The identity of an enterprise is influenced by its behaviour as a whole, but decisively by visible things." The products are especially important in this context. "The design of the products reveals whether an enter-prise is drawing on its identity or using things of alien origin. Only businesses which stand by their own guns can survive in the long term on demanding markets." The task which results is

In spite of the variety
of Rodenstock
communications topics,
a harmonisation is
achieved in design.

Concentration on the
essentials becomes
a new guiding principle
at Rodenstock AG.

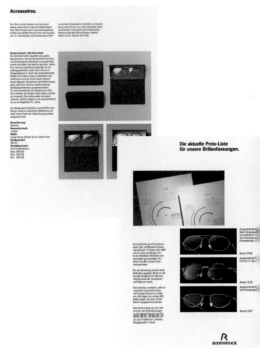

therefore "to identify and develop a design attitude in the context of the corporate identity". This is a seemingly paradoxical piece of work, whose objective is to use design to create an identity which itself has a feedback effect on the design, and so on. The paradox is however resolved as soon as the actual work starts.

The target: The target was formulated as follows: To strengthen a positive image, to promote the company's credibility and to increase the persuasive power of the brand.

The way: Rodenstock resolved to adopt the same image at all locations. "In everything Rodenstock does, aesthetics should be discernible – a cultivated type of order which makes the striving for perfection visible and credible, even in the details." This can best be achieved by an independent and meaningful design of the products and the means of communication. For its implementation, principles for communications and fundamentals of product design were set down jointly with external consultants in seminars and workshops, and systematically transformed into actions.

For product design, key concepts such as usability, quality, order, detail, proportions, longevity and context were defined, and explained and illustrated in detail in a brochure with texts and pictures. From that time on, they provided a binding guideline for product development. "A frame design that follows

Corporate communications

41

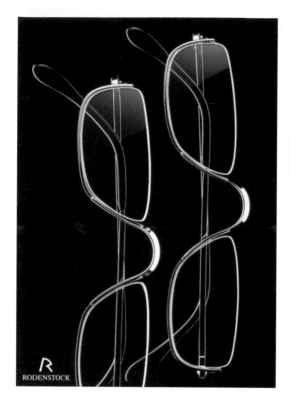

Rodenstock
demonstrates visible
perfection in
its specific product
aesthetics.

these principles will also reflect the corporate identity." This is
so, because design is understood and practised as a visual
analogy to an also reformulated scale of concepts and values
for corporate identity.

The result:
The process of identity development at Rodenstock is not yet
complete, and if it continues to be practised as it has to date,
there is probably no end in sight – much to the benefit of the
company. For that would be synonymous with a new loss of
identity. It is, then, important for this process to be continued
incessantly, following the well-known Zen dictum, "the path is
the destination". For the existence of the enterprise, it is therefore important that this path should be trodden as long as
possible.

In the Anglo-Saxon world, appearances are merely deceptive, but in an old German proverb they command respect. The latter applies without restriction to the appearance of companies on the market. Those who attach only little value to the form of their appearance have difficulty in establishing a respectable image and thus achieving a high profile. But that is more than ever before the most important condition of commercial success.

The appearance of a company is responsible to an absolutely decisive extent for its favourable image – something only one percent of German businesses would willingly do without, as a poll reveals. 83 percent of companies even think that a good image is highly important in terms of their own success. In coming to this conclusion, they are indirectly pleading for a more intensive use of design, although that has not of course come to pass as yet.

In this case, image can be defined as a positive social value which a company acquires for itself by means of a design-orientated behavioural strategy. The image of the company is first created as a self-portrait which outsiders accept as a true picture. A company can, for example, project a good impression of its corporate purpose and its products if it knows how to project itself by design. A company can be said to have an image and preserve it if its action strategy suggests a consistent personality which is confirmed by the judgements and statements of customers and other persons who do not belong to the company.

Design raises the profile

Corporate communications

Although great importance is attached to a good image, many companies do not do enough with sufficient conviction to achieve a better reputation by developing a good appearance. Not infrequently, they try to achieve a favourable market presence by means of superficial, spontaneous activities, but this is revealed on closer observation to be an illusory appeal and mere styling.

As finicky and time-consuming as it may be to construct a positive image with the aid, for instance, of design, the more promising is nevertheless the success which is sure to be achieved in the course of time. This is why companies should not waste their energy on creating a beautiful but ephemeral illusion, but devote all their strength to concentrating on long-term values and qualities.

Example
FSB Franz Schneider
Brakel GmbH & Co,
Brakel

The company: FSB is a manufacturer of door fittings, established over a century ago.

The task: As a result of the recession in the building trade, the FSB company set itself the task in the eighties of creating a new consciousness of its products and the company itself among architects, joiners and final customers, so as to emerge from its anonymity and develop a new, high profile and image. In spite of difficult market conditions, this was to assist the company in asserting itself against the competition.

The way to the solution: First step: Development of an ideal within the company as a kind of perfect self-portrait with help from external (design) consultants.

The most important step here is to clarify the kind of image the company wants for itself. Unless this is done, there is absolutely no point in involving (design) consultants to reflect on a new corporate image and a new product design. You first have to know what you want to be and what you want to do.

In this phase, it was established that FSB manufactures products for the hand, intended to be gripped and grasped. Starting from this premise, the view of the company as a whole had to be changed.

Second step: Formulation of a message and establishment of a "philosophy of gripping" as the basis of market presentation.

The FSB hand
which decorates every
catalogue from the
company.

Ludwig Wittgenstein's
door handle. The model
for the FSB logo.

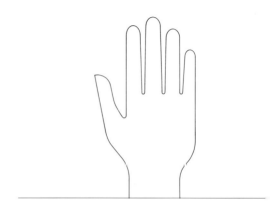

With the concentration on gripping, human beings with their genuine needs are moved into the focus of entrepreneurial interest. If door handles had previously been regarded as pure accessories without any individual raison d'être, that object obtained a completely new character of its own with this new way of seeing.

Finally, four commandments were defined in the new "philosophy of gripping", and these are now accepted throughout the industry. With this message, FSB rose to become a recognised advanced thinker in the industry.

Third step: Development and implementation of a new, design-orientated corporate strategy for product development and communications.

The strategic phase of new design management starts with the work on the product itself. Within the company, the designation "European strategy" was coined for this work. This encompassed cooperation with leading European industrial designers, so as to develop numerous new, strikingly designed products and thus achieve a better differentiation of the range and a memorable market image. With this method of product differentiation, new market shares were to be won on an extensively saturated market. The design of the FSB collection consciously moves in the field of tension between function, form and emotion.

Corporate communications

45

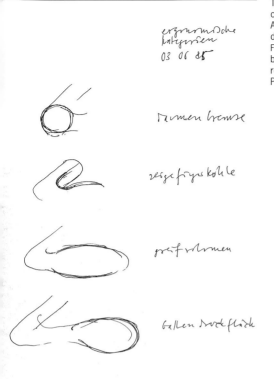

ergonomische
kategorien
03 06 85

rumen bremse

zeige finger kohle

greif volumen

fallen druck fläche

The "ergonomic categories" which Otl Aicher identified and drew, together with FSB, in 1985: Thumb brake; Index finger recess; Grip volume; Pressure surface.

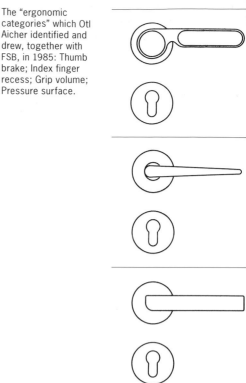

Fourth step: The sending out of advance communications to friends, customers and opinion leaders in the form of books with exemplary text and graphic design, providing information on various focal areas of the new direction FSB was to take.

Then, systematic work started on communications and image development. The self-portrait of the company thus established rapidly became an example to outside observers. With a well though-out and systematically implemented communications concept, based on the strategy of a self-fulfilling prophecy, FSB has succeeded in setting new standards for success in this field too. The communications follow the operation of a self-referring information system in which all statements refer back to themselves again and again.

Fifth step: Participation in design competitions and communication of success.

After the new self-image had been developed with great care, FSB was ready to face the verdict of the public at large. People familiar with the industry, design experts and opinion leaders were now to gain their own impressions of the company. FSB products received design awards worldwide, and the company itself also won several prizes for its design management achievements. The new FSB image became an example worthy of imitation by many other firms. Q.E.D.!

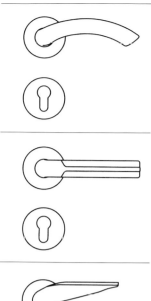

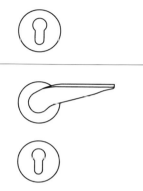

Line drawings of the "European strategy handles". The "European strategy" is the name for the development of a new design profile. Each year, a new product family is developed in cooperation with a different European designer.

The "European strategy" products also include a design by Philippe Starck.

The result: With the systematic implementation of a holistic design development strategy, FSB under the leadership of Jürgen W. Braun succeeded within only five years in moving up to occupy a pole position in the industry. At the same time, FSB thus took up a leading position on the market, firmly founded on both efficient commercial action and the new image as an avant-garde thinker. Up to now, the competition has had little to oppose this with. The work paid off: FSB has established a high profile with design!

Corporate communications

The term corporate culture is very often used as mere linguistic packaging or as a fixed and prescribed system of behaviour within a business. In consequence, entrepreneurial actions and presentations become torpid, lose their life and degenerate into compulsive, marionette-like motions. The decisive feature of this forced corporate culture is that the verbalised claims and actual appearance of the corporate culture that is lived diverge strongly from each other.

Design creates corporate culture

Culture is created by cultural behaviour. This is fundamentally determined by the crystallisation of common factors. The process involves the identification of the individual with the structures and ways of behaviour of others within a group, which themselves are distinct from those of other groups or cultures. The common factors concerned can arise in highly different fields. The important thing, however, is for common ways of thinking, seeing and acting to be developed in the selected fields, almost as a matter of course and determined independently by every individual concerned. Culture cannot, then, be defined in principle or even prescribed as a compulsive pattern of behaviour: the essential thing about it is that it is lived out voluntarily by several people in a group. Culture, in consequence, designates a specific form of life and interaction. "Cultural behaviour does not, then, arise from any particular mechanism; it merely represents a special case of communicative behaviour." (Humberto R. Maturana)

When we speak of culture in relation to a business, we mean the specific way in which the people working within it live. The role design plays in this context was once described by Otl Aicher as follows: "Design is the process of life in a business, when intentions crystallise into facts and phenomena. What people want will be made to appear. This requires the technical facilities available, but also and above all the form in which the appearance takes place. Together with the naked economics of figures, design is the substance of the business. It is not a

The standardisation and harmonisation of communications and actions by the staff in a company should be reduced to a necessary minimum so that a vital culture which creates the climate for creative and innovative achievements can develop.

mere cloak. It is the centre of the corporate culture, of innovative and creative dealings with the object of the enterprise."

As does the object of the enterprise, corporate culture ranges beyond the close boundaries of the business and its staff. The more pronounced and convincing it is, the greater its contagious appeal to outsiders whose origins are elsewhere. Cultural behaviour extends in this way to influence and superimpose itself upon the behavioural patterns of other groups or cultures. In that process, what was originally a difference can become a new common factor, gradually overcoming rigid distinctions.

For companies, this creates an opportunity to overcome the natural differences between themselves and outside associates and clients, so as to enter a common world of similar thought, perception and understanding with them. Corporate culture can thus have the power to cross borders and overcome differences in favour of its own, expanding identity. Hand in hand with that, the probability of corporate success increases.

"Persona" office chair
from Vitra GmbH.
Design: Mario Bellini
with Dieter Thiel

Wood dining chair
Design: Charles & Ray
Eames

The Vitra company manufactures and sells furniture for offices, public areas and residential accommodation.

In its history to date, Vitra has produced a corporate culture of a quite special kind, which can be observed as a living variety of complexity and contradiction. This culture is centred on design: no matter whether the issue is product development or the company's head office, internal statements, modes of behaviour or actions, or the form of the enterprise's public image, design is always given appropriate consideration in the decision-making process. In contrast to other companies, Vitra pursues a pluralistic strategy in the design of products and the architecture of corporate buildings, expressing variety rather than uniformity. The starting point for all the company's actions relevant to culture is a dialogue with creative thinkers.

Vitra products are created by designers from the four corners of the globe, by Mario Bellini (Italy), Verner Panton (Denmark), Charles Eames (USA), Jasper Morrison (England), Shiro Kuramata (Japan), Antonio Cittereo (Italy) and many, many others. As a result, many different design philosophies are conjoined in a programme of variety. The same applies to the architecture: the office and production building was designed by Nicholas Grimshaw (England), the factory by Alvaro Siza (Portugal), the fire brigade building by Zaha Hadid (Iraq) and the Vitra design museum by Frank O. Gehry (USA). The Vitra architecture defines a vital, variegated and at the same time unmistakable location for the company.

Photographer Christian Coigny never makes the prominent artists in the Vitra advertisements into mere advertisers.
Billy Wilder and Jack Lemmon

Vitra architectures define an unmistakable location of corporate culture.
Vitra fire brigade building.
Architect: Zaha Hadid

Vitra conference pavilion.
Architect: Tadao Ando

   The dialogue with the creative thinkers is also pursued beyond product design and architecture into the realm of advertising, with artists from around the world. There are now around a hundred promotional motifs from prominent artists including Miles Davis, John Cage, Audrey Hepburn, Billy Wilder, Robert Wilson and many more. Special attention is due to the style of photographer Christian Coigny, who never makes his subjects appear as mere advertisers.
   Vitra supplies an impressive example of how it is possible to create a living corporate culture with design, at the same time giving the company a strong identity and a unique appeal. This creative and innovative interaction with the object of the enterprise simultaneously ensures its commercial success.

Corporate communications

51

A large amount of money is often invested in pure advertising to establish and reinforce a brand, without taking account of the design of the products or the manufacturer's corporate image. It is not realised that a specific design attitude is essential for the creation of a brand.

Design makes brands

A branded product is always more than just an object for use in a defined application. It is also always part of an individual world view. When a product also has the property of being a brand, it distinguishes itself from all other products of the same kind and thus escapes from interchangeability. The branded product stands apart because it is capable of expressing a difference. By means of that difference, the branded product rises above the mass of products on offer, and by the same token its purchaser emerges from the crowd of anonymous consumers, entering into a community of attitude with others who purchase the product. This community distinguishes itself from other social groups, and so occupies a special position.

A branded product is what it is, because it is backed up by a particular company with its name and above all with its special attitude and aspiration to quality. And it is also essential for a brand to be unmistakable and clearly recognisable. This, again, is a function of design.

Example
C. Josef Lamy GmbH
Heidelberg

In the last 30 years, Lamy has become the leading manufacturer on the German market for high quality writing utensils. Manfred Lamy himself describes this process as "the art of putting a medium-sized business into shape". In doing so, he has succeeded in taking over not only the market leadership, but also the brand leadership. One special factor behind this success is the company's holistic orientation towards design.

In companies aiming to develop branded products, it should be ensured first and foremost that the company's image and that of its products are brought together in a carefully matched design.

Lamy 2000
Design: Gerd A. Müller
1966

Design does not play the only part in Lamy's strategic concept, but certainly a central one. "For design is an instrument in the marketing mix which can be used to demonstrate expertise and poise. Over and above that, design can be of unmatched assistance in identity-orientated communications, in the way the company presents itself." (Manfred Lamy)

The Lamy brand distinguishes itself quite strikingly from other writing utensil manufacturers in that the company has successfully established a specific Lamy design and thus an individual, corporate language of form both for the products and for the communications of the enterprise as a whole. With a uniform, easily recognisable corporate style ranging from the individual products through the packaging, the catalogues and the trade fair stands up to the architecture of the company's buildings, Lamy continuously raises its profile and becomes ever more clearly recognisable as a brand which is based on trust, liking, credibility and a constantly growing degree of familiarity. Every detail of form stands for the design approach of the whole.

The Lamy design strategy differs greatly from the Vitra concept, which proves that there are many ways to be successful with design. Many roads can lead to success, as long as it is ensured that design is practised as an operational process with strategic intent, expertise and continuity.

Lamy design is orientated towards the maxim, "form follows function". In concrete terms, this means "choosing the function,

Lamy swift
Design:
Wolfgang Fabian
1990

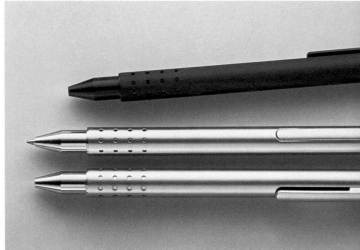

the physical usability, the technical structure of the object as the starting point, as the inspiration, as the justification for the design, with the aim of developing an ergonomically correct, functional, user-friendly product. Not only the utility quality, but also a communications quality has to be established, in order to give the product a language, make its material transparent, its engineering clear, its technical innovation visible, its handling understandable and its origin recognisable in the very physiognomy of the product by means of design". In this statement, Manfred Lamy simultaneously presents a detailed description of how brands are successfully created by design.

The Lamy brand has
established an easily
recognisable form of
corporate image,
extending from the
graphics through the
packaging to the
products themselves.

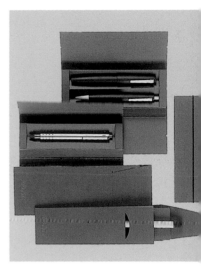

Competition on the markets of the western world is becoming ever fiercer. The development of affluence and technical progress have led to a situation in which almost every consumer need can now be satisfied by a mass of goods, hardly to be comprehended any more, to an extent which it would be difficult to exceed. This situation is leading to an extensive saturation of purchasing behaviour in more and more industries, and to a dramatic surplus in the supply of goods.

Under these market conditions, it is no longer easy to be successful with products alone, be they ever so good. Systematic pursuit of the successful marketing and sales strategies of the past is no longer anywhere near sufficient. Instead, we have to look for other opportunities and develop new strategies for sales.

The market success of a product is nowadays highly dependent on whether it can be produced – in the theatrical sense – as an event to be experienced. This goes hand in hand with a trend in market conditions away from the classical forum with a range of goods on offer, and towards a spectacular market performance. How one judges this development is of no account. Those who neglect to turn the spotlights on themselves are hardly likely to be successful.

The upshot is that it is no longer sufficient to manufacture high quality products, but it is just as important to present them in a corresponding environment. As design is playing an ever greater role in this respect, this is a further field in which it is applicable as a strategy for success.

Market +design

Marketing and sales managers are often reluctant actually to think in crazy categories and give full rein to their imagination. In consequence, they stick to the essentials of existing concepts and only modify them slightly, so – as they put it so nicely – as to bring them in line with changing market conditions. But people who always adapt too much to apparent circumstances miss the chance to do something new. Adapting means missing the boat!

New concepts

New concepts are what we need when we want to get things moving in saturated and stagnating market situations. But we only arrive at the new concepts when we are prepared to rethink and go unusual ways. The paths today's businesses tread can hardly be unusual enough, for, as management consultant Tom Peters so accurately remarks, "Crazy times call for crazy organisations". And the founder and Chief Executive Officer of Intel, a highly successful company which dominates the world market, goes even further in his latest book when he prophesies, "Only the paranoid survive".

But the pursuit of established marketing methods, complex market research projects or even spontaneous trend analyses does not enable us to be crazy enough. On the contrary, classical marketing theory, market research and the newly fashionable trend analysis only serve to draw on more or less scientific methods and discoveries to give us a reason for going on just as we were before. None of these procedures is apt to arrive at really new concepts, as they can only deal with what has gone before, what is there now, or what has already begun to take shape as a likely future.

Really new concepts, however, often arise out of a subjective antenna for new market opportunities, which I have elsewhere termed "a feeling for the market". This involves the ability to develop ideas and concepts for an emotional appeal to customers. And that requires the qualities of imagination and intuition.

Try for once to look at everything you have done up to now from an offbeat perspective. Talk to "crazy" people about new concepts. Ask yourself from time to time what your successor as general manager, marketing director or sales manager would do differently, and then do it yourself.

The company: Ritzenhoff is a long established family business which has developed in the course of the twentieth century from a traditional manufactory into one of Germany's most efficient and best known glassworks.

Example
The new concept for
RC Ritzenhoff Cristal
GmbH
Marsberg

The task: Designing a new milk glass! The Milk Marketing Association of North Rhine-Westphalia wanted to produce a "promotional glass" for milk together with glass manufacturer Ritzenhoff, "so as to put the otherwise unimposing traditional drink in the right light".

The start of the project: A brainstorming session with designers from Sieger Design, dairy managers and glass manufacturers somewhere in the country. Following that, Sieger Design develops a new product and marketing concept based on design.

The idea: Sieger Design invites well-known designers worldwide to produce a décor on the subject of milk and the glass. The only specification is a slightly conical standard glass of 12 centimetres in height. The designs are to be applied to the glass as decorations.

A special package, ideal as a gift, is designed for a set of two glasses. The selling price reflects the amount people pay on average for a good bunch of flowers. The milk glass twin pack thus becomes a brilliant idea for a present, replacing flowers or chocolates and leaving a lasting impression on those

who receive it. The glass is not so much a glass, more a gift.
That is new!

Implementation: The Milk Marketing Association is first presented with various drafts from Sieger Design with an idea for a
communications campaign and a sales strategy. Within 20
days, a total of 50 architects, designers, graphic designers and
artists are requested to take part in the project. There is an
enormous amount of interest from the designers. Too much of
a good thing for the representatives of the Milk Marketing
Association. They withdraw from the project. Ritzenhoff and
Sieger Design decide to implement the project on their own.
The first presentation takes place at the 1992 Autumn Fair in
Frankfurt.
    The first reactions are incredulous: the industry laughs.
A simple glass beaker with pretensions to design! How could
they dare...?

The result: With the implementation of the project, Ritzenhoff
achieves a hardly imaginable, unmatched market success which
is still continuing today. Since the market launch in 1992, the
glasses have produced a turnover in the tens of millions. In the
first three months alone, over 70,000 glasses were sold. Over
and above that, countless publications together with numerous
exhibitions and design awards have assured Ritzenhoff of a
worldwide reputation.

Ritzenhoff milk glass
series 1992–1996
Idea and concept:
Sieger Design

In the following years, the milk glass series is continuously
expanded with further designs. In addition, the unusual
collection is extended to cover other types of glass, like beer
and champagne glasses.

The success of a crazy idea!

Duravit, together with Hoesch and Hansgrohe (Axor), has developed a completely new product concept for bathrooms, and publicises it with great success in a persuasive promotional campaign.

Advertising with design

Design does not stop at advertising either! New concepts are of course in demand in that field too. Design can play various roles in advertising. In any case, the design of advertisements and other promotional media should be appropriate to both the company and the product advertised. The design should always reflect the corporate image of the business, and be in harmony with it.

Apart from determining the formal characteristics of an advertisement, design can also constitute a substantive statement of quality in it. The special design of a product can, for example, be explained in a text. The same applies to the promotional emphasis of product details. A reference to design awards in the advertising can also be used as an additional seal of quality.

A useful rule of thumb: The less a product differs from similar competing products in terms of technical or functional features, the more important it is for a company to differentiate itself from its competitors by an original and individual form of communication.

Advertisements are often confusing and bizarre, as a result of a visual and textual chaos in the presentation of information. Many companies follow the competition very closely in their advertising. That is why entire industries, such as the household appliances manufacturers, often present themselves in the same style with interchangeable pictures and texts. Not infrequently, companies allow themselves to become toys in the hands of the "creative" staff at their advertising agencies. Many agencies aspire to create original commercials to advertise themselves and collect their own awards, for example from the Art Directors Club. But the real interests of the client are then often neglected.

Well designed advertisements have an original aesthetic quality. They concentrate on the essentials and embody a meaningful address. Well structured information and a clear, easily readable typography demonstrate self-confidence and expertise. Unnecessary exaggerations should be totally avoided. Also, have the courage to resist ephemeral design fashions in your advertising. Instead, develop your own style. Be cautious in your dealings with advertising agencies which take their own ideas more seriously than the products of their clients. Take an active part yourself in the development of advertising concepts, instead of just waiting to be served by your agency. Take on the full responsibility for your advertising yourself!

The initial position: The job concerns the manufacture and sale of a new product in the sanitary sector. Three manufacturers of different types of sanitary ware – Hansgrohe, a maker of fittings and bathroom accessories, Hoesch, the manufacturer of baths, whirlpools and shower basins, and Duravit, who produce bathroom fittings, furniture and accessories – resolve to cooperate to achieve something the industry has never seen before. Jointly, they appoint the star designer Philippe Starck to design a completely fitted out new bathroom from a single pair of hands.

Example
A new cooperation
concept by
Hansgrohe (Axor),
Hoesch
and Duravit

Product design: Philippe Starck begins to rethink the things in the bathroom from fundamental principles. In doing so, he draws on associations from a time long past, when the water was still fetched from the earth with a pump and poured into a bowl for washing, when people still sat on a pail and took their baths in a trough. The images of this history can make memories come alive in everyone. Starck used them to design, as a metamorphosis, a completely recreated bathroom. The design of each individual product is reminiscent of an original form from the past. Starck combines his design concept with a history which everyone can easily understand and which is in addition graphically demonstrable.

Market appearance: Three companies work together to launch the new bathroom product ensemble on the market. This

Market

becomes possible because all three can tell the same story and, in Philippe Starck, all three have the same person to identify with. Their actions thus gain in authenticity. The competition is skeptical, and sees little prospect of the project being successful. Today, the "Starck bathroom" has become a trauma for many competitors, as its success has been colossal.

A decisive factor behind this success is the joint market presence of the three companies, enabling them to triple their communications potential, for example in advertising. There is also threefold strength behind the sales of the products. But the greatest role is played by the historical allusion, which provides a framework for a product performance rich in experience. The new bathroom is not presented in simple salesrooms, of course, but staged like a piece of theatre. The advertising serves to announce the restaging of the bathroom in an aesthetically perfect form as the premiere of a new play which no-one should miss.

Success then comes about seemingly automatically. Entire audiences view the scenario with interest, and many feel tempted to enter into the events themselves. A new concept and advertising with design have truly paid off!

In the world of perfume, packaging is decisive for the success of the product. Design: Peter Schmidt Studios for Joop

Seduction by packaging

It is no longer sufficient merely to produce well designed products. They also have to be communicated, in the right aesthetic setting and with emotional appeal. It is the design of the product periphery, then, that will continuously gain in importance as a factor behind future market success. Packaging deserves special attention. Not infrequently, it decides the success or failure of a well designed product. The first contact with the customer takes place as a rule via the packaging.

A general rule: There are no second chances if first impressions are bad.

In many cases, packaging allows customers to get their bearings and gives them confidence. Forty percent of all women, for example, cannot recognise their perfume without its packaging. The eye rules not only over the sense of smell, but also over taste.

Just as there are specialists in product and graphic design, so there are those who specialise in the design of packaging. Businesses should not let these reserves of expertise go untapped. One of these specialists who sets new standards in the field again and again is the Hamburg-based designer Peter Schmidt, one of whose packages surely everyone has at some time held in their hands. From Milka chocolate through Jacobs coffee and Deinhard sparkling wine, to the humble mineral water bottle, he and his team have helped at least one company from almost every product segment to success with their out-

**Example
Peter Schmidt
Studios
Hamburg**

Market

Problem Companies often fail to make the effort to develop suitable packaging for their products. The result is a significant restriction of their own competitive position on the market.

Recommendation Design is not only of great importance in product development and in corporate communications: product packaging should also be designed in such a way that it facilitates a clear communicative identification with the product at all times.

standing design. The designs from the Peter Schmidt studio are in especially great demand in the fashion and perfume industries.

In Peter Schmidt's view, his work revolves around wrapping an object so as to make it visible. The knack consists in seducing the prospective customers in a charming and unobtrusive way, awaking their desire to see the contents of the packaging. Often enough, the packaging itself becomes an object of desire, which in this case, in contrast to advertising, is thoroughly permissible, as when the packaging is purchased the product also changes hands. In Peter Schmidt's design, it is not artistic aesthetics or any particular style that count, but the decisive factor is the effect alone, and that is not revealed solely by design prizes, but above all by sales success.

Example
Simon & Goetz
Frankfurt

A vivid example of how important it is for companies to develop new concepts in the packaging of their products is provided by the communications agency Simon & Goetz of Frankfurt with their development of a new brand image and packaging concept for Fichtel & Sachs Zweiradtechnik. The latter company is a manufacturer of bicycle components, such as gear systems, wheels, hubs, sprockets and so on. The traditional image of the long-established company stood, from a present point of view, for reliability and quality, but not for up to date solutions, or indeed for innovation.

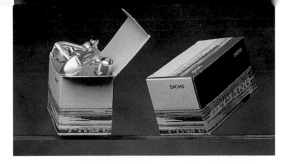

With the new concept, Simon & Goetz succeeded to a remarkable degree in laying the foundation stone for a favourable transformation of the Fichtel & Sachs image. The heart of the concept is the idea of "easy movement", which is systematically implemented in a packaging design for the products with associations of lightness and dynamism.

Simon & Goetz were awarded the Grand Prix in the German Prize for Communications Design for their exemplary achievement in 1996. The courage exhibited by Fichtel & Sachs was rewarded with a significant improvement in their market position.

Constructiv "Pila" trade
fair system:
Design: Burkhardt
Leitner constructiv

Trade fairs need design

For a long time, trade fair stands and salesrooms were regarded merely as a necessary means towards an end, requiring
no particular design preparation. Today, things are different.
With an increasing pressure of competition and the expansive
range of products on offer, it has become important to stage the
right product performances for every location. And the places
where products are sold are, of course, at the top of the bill.

Trade fair stands and salesrooms are nowadays venues for
communication. A convincing, well thought-out and emotionally
appealing design can project a message promoting identification with a company and its products even as a prospective
customer enters these areas. If this is to be achieved, all the
elements of design, from the architecture to the furnishings and
communications materials must be in harmony with the design
concept for the company and its products.

Exhibition and presentation systems play a special role.
When deployed at trade fairs in particular, these systems have
to satisfy special demands in terms of form and function.
On the one hand, it is important for them to provide an aesthetic
variety of potential configurations, and on the other hand
they have to be easy to handle, shortening setting up and taking
down times, and thus saving not only time but also money.

Burkhardt Leitner, the designer from Stuttgart, has formulated the following four essential design criteria for a good trade fair and exhibition system:

1. Visual identification: The system must provide for a broad range of individual configurations by using various materials, colours and system structures. This facilitates the design of a memorable space which makes individual and original company and product presentations possible.

2. Flexibility: The greatest possible freedom in planning must be allowed, for reaction to different occasions and circumstances. In addition, the transformation of individual elements should ensure an aesthetic appearance throughout a long service life of the system.

3. Functionality: The system must, of course, fulfil technical, functional and stability requirements to perfection. A high degree of modularity and self-explanatory components are important prerequisites for rapid assembly and dismantling.

4. System communication/Product communication: The system must itself be clearly structured, just as it should be capable of supporting product communications with optimum display facilities. For this purpose, it must be possible to integrate con-

Market

Companies invest large sums in spectacular trade fair appearances without taking account of the overall design image of the business on the market. This often leads to inelegant presentations with no credibility.

Use only a few structural components to create a maximum of presence and atmosphere, in harmony with the holistic design philosophy of your enterprise.

temporary means of communication such as CAD, CD-ROM or video without difficulty.

To date, Burkhardt Leitner has demonstrated the fulfilment of these criteria with his systems for many companies, including AEG, BMW, Audi, Lufthansa and the Frankfurt Trade Fair Organisation.

Design-orientated businesses, no matter which industry they belong to, represent an attraction and a focal point for the visitors at every trade fair. The main events at many trade fairs are concentrated around the stands of companies like this. Trade fair organisers are also aware that design can make a major contribution to the success of their activities. That is why they tend from time to time to use design-orientated businesses almost as bait to catch other, less or not design-orientated businesses as exhibitors. Many design-orientated companies regard this practice, which is particularly prevalent at furniture, jewellery or household appliance fairs, as detrimental and disruptive. For that reason, these companies search for alternative exhibition concepts and presentation venues where they can present themselves and their products undisturbed by less qualified manufacturers.

At the Design Zentrum Nordrhein Westfalen, we responded to this kind of situation among the existing jewellery fairs by creating a separate, high quality exhibition forum for design-orientated jewellery manufacturers. Under the name of

selection98
schmuck, uhren
und objekte

"selection", a new, annual form of presentation for selected jewellery manufacturers and design-orientated dealers was called to life for the first time in 1998. The event was immediately a great success: many of the exhibitors accepted the alternative and turned their backs on the conventional trade fair business. In addition, they did better business, because the around 10,000 interested visitors to the fair brought numerous new business contacts to many of the exhibitors.

Example
Design Zentrum
Nordrhein Westfalen
Essen

Respo

Entrepreneurial action is always responsible action, as otherwise the survival of the company would not be possible. Those who act as entrepreneurs at least take on the responsibility for their own actions, although this does not always mean that they act responsibly towards other people and their environment.

Those, however, who are aiming at permanent success and the survival of their businesses in the long term, can only achieve those aims when they accept responsibility on the way there not only for themselves, but also for their fellow human beings and the environment. For entrepreneurial success always presupposes action in the context of society and the environment.

In this respect, all entrepreneurial action has an ethical significance, for it is action which contributes to the creation of the world in which we live. The shape and quality of this world is decisively determined by the nature of that action. Design can take on a fundamental role here, when an improvement in the quality of life and the environment is to be achieved. This objective is pursued by more and more companies today, which itself shows how important it is to reflect on various ways of applying design in this connection too.

For a business entity, design-orientated action means that it is consciously involved in a special, creative way in the establishment of high quality living conditions.

The world we live in does not exist independently of our actions. On the contrary, we are ourselves part of the continuous process of changing and regenerating it and our responsibility is correspondingly great.

The creation of every new product entails a decision as to how it will change our lives. This is a responsibility that cannot be evaded and industry has a duty in this respect that far exceeds the duty of the individual. The design decisions made by companies will significantly change our world for better or worse. Irresponsible design can cost all of us far more than is at first apparent.

Entrepreneurs often think that ecological actions lead to losses. They feel justified in this attitude as long as other businesses in global competition neglect to behave in an ecological manner. They are not, then, prepared to take on responsibility themselves in this field, but rather procrastinate and make their own actions dependent on the actions of others. This attitude is not, however, indicative of entrepreneurial consciousness, but rather of negligence in preparing for the future of the company, which is itself decisively dependent on the quality of the environment.

The environment

In Taipei, in 1995, during my heynote-speech at the ICSID Congress, I asked many hundreds of designers from across the globe questions like these: How green is your design? Would you be prepared to design non-ecological products? Have you ever rejected a commission because your conscience troubled you?

I was horrified by the audience's reaction. Not one of the designers present was willing to answer these questions or devote more attention to the problems addressed.

Design and ecology appear initially to be diametrically opposed. After all, in an ideal case, design is supposed to create usable and attractive products for the users, thus increasing the sales figures and maximising the profits of the manufacturer. On the other hand, companies which act responsibly are nowadays called upon to accept an appropriate degree of responsibility for the environment. The contradiction between design and ecology can therefore only be resolved inasfar as design can be integrated in an ecologically responsible business management. Where this is possible, designers will also be able to afford to refuse commissions to design ecologically unconscionable products. In recent years, a certain amount of progress has been made in this respect.

Rome was not built in a day. The first small steps on the way towards an ecologically responsible enterprise can be taken, for example, by asking yourself whether there are really no ecologically and at the same time economically justifiable alternatives to what you currently do. As soon as you begin to see that some things might be done differently, you are on the right track.

"Picto" office chair: Ecological responsibility in product design. Design: Produktentwicklung Roericht (B. Schmitz/ F. Biggel)

Recognition: "At Wilkhahn, no two bricks are to be put together any longer unless ecology and economics, aesthetics and human aspects are in harmony in the building they create."

(Fritz Hahne, co-owner of Wilkhahn, in a memo dating from 1984)

Example
Steps towards
ecological change
at Wilkhahn
Bad Münder

The company: Wilkhahn is a manufacturer of furniture for offices and conference rooms, and for public areas. The company not only ranks among the pioneers of design development in Germany, but is now also regarded as a leader in the implementation of ecological design concepts. Ecology is an important part of the corporate philosophy at Wilkhahn.

In 1996, Wilkhahn was awarded the German Environment Prize for ecological business management.

The task: An environmental strategy was to be integrated in the corporate planning. "What we need is not just a bit more conservation, but a fundamental reorientation of the entire company and its products, leading to constant improvements in their ecological soundness."

The way: 1st step: Firstly, all the staff have to be involved in the process. This requires transparency of the ecological concept.

2nd step: Establishment of environmental controlling. On the basis of a definition of the corporate ecological objectives, the

Responsibility

Priorities in the use of
materials at Wilkhahn,
using the "Picto" office
chair as an example.

With the "Conrack"
development, Wilkhahn
proves that ecological
design concepts are
thoroughly capable of
satisfying contem-
porary demands on the
top floor.
Design: Wiege Entwick-
lungsgesellschaft

task of the environmental controlling system is to detect and
evaluate ecological weaknesses in the company, and to develop
firm plans to improve the situation.

In addition, an ecological balance sheet is compiled, providing an overview in the form of an input-output analysis of the
works.

3rd step: Integration of the ecological knowledge in the
company's workflows by more intensive involvement of the staff.
Workgroups are set up to establish and organise ecological
knowledge in the sectors of production, materials management,
information systems, organisation and communication.

4th step: Implementation and realisation of the identified ecological improvements and performance of ongoing training and
qualification schemes with the staff. Development and production of new ecological products. Continuous updating of the
environmental programme.

Repair for the customer

Return

Recycling, re-use of parts

Orderly disposal

Ecologically conscious project office planning: At Wilkhahn, a furnishing culture which allows the 40 year old "Programm 400" to blend perfectly with the latest product developments like "Confair" and "Logon" has developed.

Product design: The traditional specifications of form and function are now accompanied by a further one: environmental compatibility. Its criteria are
– durability,
– priority for natural, regenerating raw materials,
– economical material input,
– appropriateness of materials,
– unmixed materials,
– recyclability,
– environmentally sound consumables,
– material marking,
– detachable joints,
– repair friendliness, ease of dismantling,
– products free from emissions.

The impact of product design is also considered above and beyond the processes of production and distribution, into the phases of use and what happens after use.

Responsibility

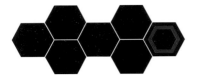  

Use

There are things that function perfectly, but are hard to use. Handling products like video recorders, computers and technical equipment of all kinds is tantamount to a daily intelligence test. It is use that finally determines whether a product is well designed or not. It is by no means the least important function of design to optimise the utility properties of a product. This can be done in various ways:

- by providing the product with a comprehensible, easily controlled user interface,
- by clear and easily understandable product graphics,
- by good workmanship,
- by the design of plausible operating instructions.

Good design not only creates beautiful products, but also the conditions for good handling of them. The usefulness of a product is always the result of its application and use.

With many companies, the customer is only king before the product is bought, and then becomes a beggar. Elaborate, well designed information material is deployed to promote the sale. After purchasing, the customer has to make do with neglectfully designed and hardly comprehensible instruction manuals.

Many companies devote too little attention to optimising the utility properties of their products and thus ensuring customer satisfaction after the purchase.

Product design should not only focus on technical and functional perfection, but also on the optimisation of use. This entails in particular a good design of the operating instructions, which are regarded by law in many countries as an integral part of the product.

With the glass ceramic honeycomb hob, designer Klaus Keichel and the Küppersbusch project team redefined the use of the cooker.

The company: Küppersbusch started manufacturing cookers for households and restaurants as early as 1875, over 120 years ago, and the company still manufactures kitchen equipment for professional and private use.

Example
Reflections on the
use of cookers
at Küppersbusch AG
Gelsenkirchen

The initial situation: There is a realisation at Küppersbusch that more will have to be done in future to ensure a continuous improvement in product quality. The background is a desire to keep out of price competition, as Küppersbusch, one of the last medium sized businesses in the industry, would not have a chance of surviving in the long term against the major companies with their significantly larger production runs. As a result, far better opportunities are seen in competition through quality, and a decision is taken to adopt that strategy. But how can the firm get even better than it already is? Finally, an important opportunity is identified in taking on further responsibility vis-à-vis the customer by means of the design of the products.

The way: The general management and product managers from Küppersbusch AG make contact with the Design Zentrum Nordrhein Westfalen, with a view to examining improvement strategies in product design together with my staff and myself.

1st step: Staff from the two organisations form a joint project group which intensively examines the history of cookers, their development and utility function.

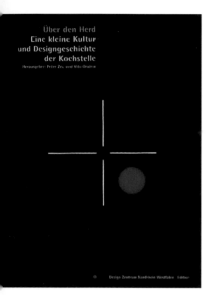

Über den Herd
Eine kleine Kultur
und Designgeschichte
der Kochstelle

Herausgeber: Peter Zec und Vitu Oralien

Design-Zentrum Nordrhein Westfalen Editor

The publication,
"On Stoves", documents
the Küppersbusch
study on a new culture
of cooking.

One result is that insufficient attention has been paid so far to the design of use in the development of stoves.

2nd step: It is important for the company's customers to become involved in this development process. The decision is therefore taken to perform a study on cookers which is to define the criteria of use for a good stove. In the course of that study, customers of the company, professional and amateur chefs, designers, architects, experts on nutrition and journalists are asked about how they use cookers. In addition, work studies are performed.

3rd step: The study is then documented in the form of a book, "On Stoves", and published.
In parallel with the study, new product concepts are developed and made ready for marketing. The first result is a glass ceramic honeycomb hob which makes cooking with several pans much easier by ensuring greater flexibility in use.

4th step: The results of the project work are presented to dealers and discussed with them in seminars. The continuous process of improvement is pursued in dialogues with customers, cooks, designers and architects.

Recaro Style retrofit
car seat (1996)
Recaro GmbH & Co,
Kirchheim/Teck
In-house design:
Bernd Rager,
Frank Beermann,
Dieter Armbrecht

"sacco" seat (1970)
Piero Gatti, Cesare
Paolini and Franco
Teodoro for Zanotta,
Milan.

Health

Design practised responsibly must also pay special regard to
the health of the users. Wherever people are in contact
with equipment for relatively long periods, sitting, gripping or
viewing, special ergonomic principles have to be taken into
account in the design of the products. Ideally, the specific
needs and behavioural patterns of human beings are reflected
in the product design. The designer becomes a design
engineer, incorporating people in the product as an integral
part of the system.

But ergonomically orientated design is not synonymous with
adapting the product to the shape of the human body. On the
contrary, the aim is to design products in such a way that there
is as little strain as possible in using them and that no physical
wear is caused.

The "sacco" seat manufactured by Zanotta does of course
snugly adjust to any posture, but people who have "sat" on it
quickly realise that maximum adjustment to the shape of the
human body does not always fulfil the criteria of ergonomics.

Example
Sacco

Exactly the opposite is the case with the Recaro automobile
sports seat. Even if it does not seem as comfortable as the
"seat bag", its design with organic overtones nevertheless
expresses a striving for optimum sitting comfort. The seat is
notable for its high ergonomic standard. The shoulder pad provides additional support when driving. Furthermore, the wings

Example
Recaro automobil
sports seat

Responsibility

After numerous tests
had been performed,
the design concept for
this miracle of comfort
was finally developed.
"Aeron" office swivel
chair (1994)
Herman Miller, Zeeland
MI, USA
Design: Bill Stumpf,
Don Chadwick

on the backrest and the seat extension for thigh support, in
conjunction with a climatisation system in the seat cushion and
backrest, ensure a pleasant and relaxing posture during long
drives.

Ten finger typing on conventional keyboards brings the
arms together at an angle of around 30° in front of the body, and
the wrists are therefore always in a slightly stressed position
relative to the keyboard. In the long term, this can lead to wear
on the joints and sinews. Apple Computer solved this problem
by designing an ergonomic, individually adjustable keyboard.

**Example
Aeron swivel
office chair**

The "Aeron" swivel office chair, designed by Don Chadwick
and Bill Stumpf in 1994, was designed on an ergonomic basis
following numerous tests. It is a chair in three sizes, just as
suitable for a dainty female frame as for a man over six feet tall.

The designers incorporated prophylactic properties in the
"Aeron" which ensure that the body remains relaxed and
the sitter feels good even in phases of intensive work with great
concentration.

Instead of the conventional foam and fabric upholstery, a
breathing pellicle membrane is used. The chair also has a tilt
function.

Design is not always practised with due consideration for health. Sometimes, manufacturers follow the trends of fashion in their product development, implementing striking stylistic features at the expense of ergonomic concerns.

Manufacturers of equipment and objects which are intended for relatively intensive use in the household, at the workplace or in the fields of leisure and sports, should take care in the design of those products to keep physical wear as a consequence of using the products as low as possible. Better market success can also be achieved with this qualitative advantage.

Long-lived products are particularly robust and durable in use. Long life is a special product quality, very often aimed at by manufacturers and designers, but by no means always achieved.

One thing is however certain: the achievement of long life in a product presupposes responsible action by all those involved in the development and manufacturing process.

Long-lived products do not only differ from short-lived products in that they are offered on the market for longer. Above all, they are characterised by several or even all of the following criteria:

– sound manufacturing quality,
– use of low-wear materials,
– good provision for maintenance and repairs,
– a high degree of practicality,
– resistance to misuse,
– the ability to be refilled or upgraded,
– a long-lived language of form,
– unspectacular but appropriate colour scheme,
– design originality.

Why is it worthwhile aiming at durability for products? Because long-lived products prove extremely advantageous in a variety of ways: for the manufacturer, who saves costs and makes higher profits in the long term; for the purchaser, who can use the product for longer and thus saves the money which would

Companies very often follow the behaviour patterns of their competitors and fail to concentrate on developing their own original product concepts aimed at long-term success rather than boosting earnings in the short term.

Have the courage to develop "design classics", and do everything you can to position them on the market in the long term.

WMF salt and pepper shakers "Max und Moritz" (1952)
The product, developed in the early nineteen-fifties, has remained in production ever since. A real icon of long life in product design.
WMF Württembergische Metallwarenfabrik AG, Geislingen/Steige
Design: Prof. Wilhelm Wagenfeld

otherwise have been spent on new purchases; for the environment, which is polluted less, because durable products do not have to be disposed of so quickly.

There is no firm rule as to how long a product has to be on the market to be regarded as long-lived. In industries which are highly responsive to fashion and innovation, such as the photographic and home electronics sectors, a product can be termed long-lived after only a few years, because it has lost nothing of its power to survive in the face of numerous new, competing products. In contrast, products like tools and machines usually only achieve the status of longevity after many years, because they were designed for long-term use and the competition requires longer cycles to put innovations on the market.

In 1978, the designer Rido Busse inaugurated a design competition in which products which had been successful on the market for eight years and in addition exhibited good design were distinguished by a "Longlife Design Award".

Prof. Wilhelm Wagenfeld designed many long-lived products for WMF. This is further proof that investing in good design is worthwhile.

Example
WMF
Württembergische
Metallwaren AG
Geislingen/Steige
One company which has a multitude of long-lived products is Württembergische Metallwarenfabrik AG, better known by its abbreviation WMF, in Geislingen/Steige. WMF products in general stand for robustness, low-wear materials, a durable language of form, and a high degree of practicality and design originality. It is particularly remarkable that WMF persistently and purposefully backed the concept of long life even during a period in which the design of table accessories took on new, spectacular and trendy features again and again. The precise opposite is Alessi from Italy, who made a major contribution to the degeneration of the language of form of products for the dinner table in the eighties. At that time, WMF succeeded in an astounding manner in resisting the pressure of competition. Even today, the company has bestsellers which were created during that period.

The design of most WMF products is, even if the term had come into some disrepute in the meantime, timeless and orientated towards practicality and functional use. In this respect, the company is located within the globally acclaimed German design tradition which started with the Deutscher Werkbund and the Bauhaus and extends into the present via the Hochschule für Gestaltung in Ulm. One WMF product has earned special attention in this regard. It is the "Max und Moritz" salt and pepper set designed by Wilhelm Wagenfeld, which has been in production continuously since 1952 and is still successful on the market even after 45 years. At the time it was developed,

Rice and serving spoon, designed by Carl Pott. A design classic, available in the C. Hugo Pott GmbH range for 30 years now.

The best prospects for a new, long-lived product family: "Picado" parmesan knife
Design: Ralph Krämer

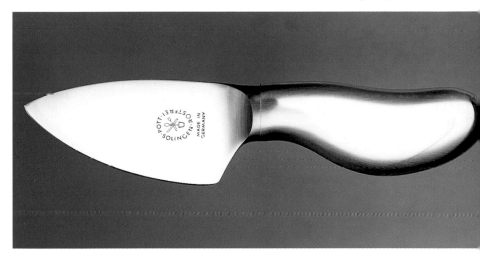

the product presented a real manufacturing problem, as the high precision metal cap had to be clipped onto a glass component with large tolerances. Both Wilhelm Wagenfeld, sadly long departed, and WMF, have achieved a real "design classic" with this product.

It is certainly not a matter of chance that another metalworking company has also written design history with its long-lived products, all of which are still on the market today. Here, we are talking about cutlery manufacturer Carl Hugo Pott from Solingen. The design of the Pott cutlery also follows the philosophy of the Bauhaus. Although a number of product designs clearly reveal traces of their origins, they have lost nothing of their aesthetic appeal even today, and continue to appear modern. The company's more recent products, too, already reveal a propensity to long life.

Example
C. Hugo Pott GmbH
Solingen

Responsibility

Design is nowadays becoming increasingly important in the media, above all for television stations and magazines. This is because the media too, no matter whether printed or audio-visual in nature, are exposed to an increasing pressure of competition and therefore have to stand their ground as products on the market. The times when the media occupied a special monopoly-like position in our society are definitely past.

With the introduction of private television in 1984, when RTL started broadcasting to Germany, an enormous surge was felt throughout the German media landscape. Within a relatively short period, numerous new products appeared on the television and magazine markets, becoming more and more similar in what they had to offer. The more similar these media products become in terms of content, the more their external form determines their market success or failure. It is not, of course, possible to package television programmes or magazines in the way to which we have become accustomed with other products, but they do at least require a comparable form of presentation if they are to attract our attention. This, once again, is a task for design.

Trends and movements in magazine or audio-visual media design often become models for advertising agencies, who recommend their clients to design their advertisements, business reports, videos or trade magazines in a similar way. But tread cautiously on this path! A good image, developed with great care, can be rapidly ruined by adapting to fashionable trends in communications and so diluting an established identity.

Media +design

Poster for the "Design Innovations '93" exhibition at the Design Zentrum Nordrhein Westfalen.
Design: André Maassen
Photo: Hans Hansen

Poster for the European Design Congress "Design – quo vadis? New tools and strategies for the European design of the future". Design Zentrum NRW, 1992.
Design: Uwe Loesch

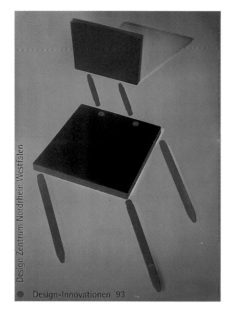

Posters

The function of posters is first and foremost that of signalling. They are either intended to draw attention to an event, such as a concert, an exhibition or some other kind of meeting, or to advertise a product or service. Or they aim to stir memories of past events. In any case, they always have to be capable of appealing to an observer in the fleeting encounter of an instant. Only when the observer perceives the message and understands what it means can we assume that communication between the poster and the observer has taken place. Comprehension is always a necessary condition.

This comprehension can manifest itself in a variety of ways: as agreement, as questioning or as rejection. The important thing is however for one of these consequent operations in the communications process to take place in the observer's mind.

Posters are capable of producing such an instantaneous effect on the observer when they are designed in such a way as to stand out in a clearly perceptible manner from their surroundings. Or in other words, posters must be distinguishable and thus easily recognisable by the observer. It is certainly not always necessary for everything written on a poster to be clearly legible from far away. The only really decisive factor is for an overall communicative effect to be achieved. After all, when the first appeal has been understood, it may well be possible for people to move closer to the poster and take their time reading the small print.

In many cases, posters are over-loaded with text information, leading to total incomprehension on the part of the observer. Posters sometimes also have a loud, inappropriate design that only produces a kind of shock effect. But shocks as a rule do very little to promote comprehension by the observer.

In the design of posters, "less is more" is the principle to follow. A clear and simple typographic design should blend aesthetically with the graphical level.

The design quality of a poster is especially dependent on the manner in which a relationship is established between the typography and the graphics. This demands a certain flair which not every art director or graphic designer possesses. There are some designers who have developed an outstanding sensitivity in poster design. These are the specialists who should be approached when the scene is to be set on billboards for events or products.

Media

Printed media

Not only the journalistic component, but also the design is of major significance in determining the success or failure of today's magazines. Once again, the competitive situation on the market, at the news agent's or in canvassing for subscribers is decisive. Various trends in the design of magazines can be observed at present, all of which however, irrespective of the design elements they use, are aimed at accelerating reading and perception. Magazine design is thus determined more and more by the perception behaviour we develop in our dealings with audio-visual media. Sections of text are then either clearly structured and easily identifiable, so that they can be read very rapidly, or they are accelerated into total illegibility by a pictorial typography.

The design of "Focus" magazine is a very good example of the first case. The magazine's rapid market success in spite of the strong competition from the established magazine "Spiegel" supplies convincing evidence of how important design now is to magazines. In order to assert its position against Focus, Spiegel had to react with a new design. The weekly newspapers "Die Zeit" and "Die Woche" are also facing each other in a similar competitive duel, although in this case the latter has a much more convincing design, which is reflected not least in its greater commercial success.

The experiment with "Fuse", the interactive magazine developed by Neville Brody in 1990 is a characteristic example of the second case. Fuse, the medium for experimental typography,

conveys no content other than itself, and permits a free play
with letters and typefaces. Brody regards it as an abstract typography which is at the same time a liberation from content and
meaning.

Together with Neville Brody, the American David Carson has
also caused a worldwide furore with his specific style of magazine design. Even the publishers of Die Zeit's magazine were
unable to withstand the seductive fascination of the design
spectacle, and engaged the typography guru to design issue
no. 23 of 31st May 1996.

It would have been better for them if they hadn't. For the
Zeit magazine designed by Carson demonstrates right down to
the smallest detail that it is simply impossible to find a common
denominator between a conservative editorial concept and
an expressive, avant-garde design. The result is simultaneously
absurd and scurrilous. Only the Apple computer company was
able to see any sense in it. In a clearly legible advertisement
on the inner back cover of the magazine, the company thanked
David Carson for "producing 39 pages of advertising for us".
He had, after all, shown with his design what fantastic things
can be done with a graphics program from Apple Computer.

Media

At its home page, the Design Zentrum Nordrhein Westfalen offers a virtual tour through the International Design Exhibition in Essen. Design: Una-Design

Just as the term multimedia is firmly established nowadays, the design problems that occur in this new field of communications are also firmly established. The difficulty is that there is neither a new patent recipe nor any tried and tested procedural patterns for the design of multimedia presentations – either on a CD-ROM or in the Internet. There is, then, still unlimited freedom for creative experimentation. As much as this may please a new generation of multimedia designers, it is just as problematical for companies developing presentations in this field, because they cannot afford to miss out on a prompt positioning in the virtual space of communications.

One special creative challenge in the handling of multimedia for all those involved is whether and how communications in virtual space can be given a real meaning. This challenge faces not only designers, but also all those who commission design services. They too should devote intensive thought to what exactly they want to do and how they can best do it.

Many companies still only post the same texts and designs as they use in their printed media on their home pages in the Internet. They are also frequently unclear about who they really want to communicate with in the Internet and how best to do so. Do we want to use the Internet to make contact with people from the four corners of the globe who do not know us yet, or is our home page to be designed first and foremost as a prestige object for those who have known us for a long time already? Perhaps we even want to do both. It is however important to

Many companies only deal half-heartedly with multimedia applications, if at all. This can lead to considerable strategic disadvantages in future when they suddenly realise what new market opportunities the Internet and other multimedia applications can offer.

Even if there is very little experience within the organisation with regard to successful multimedia applications, there is still a real need to start gathering that experience and skill in handling them now. It is helpful to seek the assistance of designers who have specialised in this field. Information on these can be found, for instance, in the International Yearbook of Communication Design (see literature references in the appendix). Regular reading of specialist journals is also recommended.

get this clear, so that there are at least a few fundamental points of reference for the design.

A further challenge for companies is that of maintaining their usual image, and thus their corporate identity and familiar profile in the Internet. Perhaps it might even be advisable to change these to reflect the new form of communication. This however requires intensive critical consideration of the new opportunities on offer. In any case, if the venture is to be successful, it is important for the Internet and the associated multimedia applications to be regarded as an opportunity for the future of the business and not as a necessary evil or an unwelcome compulsory exercise.

The design

Laymen sometimes even have more fantastic ideas of how design is created than many designers actually like to suggest. The vision is evoked of the creative genius sitting in an aircraft, taking a shower, going for a walk or just lying on the lawn, and suddenly he is inspired with the brilliant idea for a new product which he only has to jot down as a rapid sketch – and the design of a lawn mower or electric shaver or whatever is complete.

Those who think that is true are far removed from the actual work of the designer. For product design is as a rule created in a highly complex process which in most cases follows the same pattern and is divided into various phases or development steps. Development of the design is integrated in the overall development process for the product.

The design process does not merely revolve around strivings to make a product beautiful. The aim is rather to take special account of opportunities presented by the engineering process and establish cost-effective production sequences. In the ideal case, the designer, in cooperation with engineers and marketing specialists, assists in reducing the manufacturing costs of a new product while keeping its utility value constant, or enhancing its utility value and sales potential with constant manufacturing costs. The decision on which route to take is as a rule taken in the course of the design process which is integrated in product development. The abilities of a professional designer, then, include a pronounced cost consciousness just as much as a well-founded understanding of engineering details and an aesthetic sense for the formal design.

Using the example of the design development of the mc 6 laboratory system for manufacturer Waldner, the following is a glimpse of how a design process is structured at the moll design. reiner moll & partner studio.

The client:
WALDNER Laboreinrichtungen GmbH & Co, Wangen im Allgäu.

The designer:
moll design. reiner moll & partner, Schwäbisch Gmünd
Reiner Moll and his team rank among the most creative minds in German design.

The job:
Development of a new, complex laboratory system
The development period:
5 years, (1992–1997)
The project description:
A report from moll design. reiner moll & partner.

W90, the predecessor
range from Waldner

Great freedom from above

The mc 6 laboratory system comprises all the products and components necessary for the equipping and operation of a wide range of laboratories.

All the individual components were newly designed in the course of this development and harmonised within the overall conceptual and formal strategy, so that each individual component fulfils and symbolises its purpose optimally alone and within the overall context.

Working environments change. Requirement profiles are redefined, and the move towards variable workplace structures is becoming apparent in the most divergent fields. In laboratories too, more flexible ways of use will increasingly prevail.

Drafts of the new laboratory situation

Static structures, resulting from fixed media supplies and traditional planning, have up to now dominated the laboratory landscape. Linear benches, single and double, with the work surfaces and sinks, are just as standard as Spartan analysis workplaces. In comparison with other sectors, like that of office furnishings for example, the formal and functional quality characteristics are conservative and traditional. Compare the furniture with the ultra-modern electronic equipment used on it, and the discrepancy between this field and that of office furnishings in terms of customisation for a particular profession becomes blatantly obvious.

In laboratories, both physical and mental work is performed. Systematic working procedures require a smooth flow of information. The activities are characterised by dynamic movement on the one hand, and static postures of standing and sitting on the other. Furthermore, a shift in the sterile laboratory environment towards emotionality and humanisation is desirable in the spirit of psychic ergonomics, fulfilling people's needs for communication, safety and well-being to a greater extent than in the past.

The first 1:5 scale model of the new system

In spite of demands for versatility in use, the practice to date has been to lay permanent, structurally fixed power and media supply lines, thus limiting the capacity to accommodate changes in working processes. If, as was customary in the past, all the "cells" were equipped with all the necessary media, this did permit free working throughout the standardised line, but at the same time it constituted logistical redundancy. The "versatility" was therefore achieved by costly duplication, and the fixed installations did nothing to relieve the impression of a static solution.

The logical, futuristic design response to the problem is a new media supply system based on the creation of a wing-like supporting structure which is suspended from the ceiling and can be configured in any way with the media supply facilities required. A fundamentally new supply structure with modular components provides for individual positioning of equipment and materials and the flexible arrangement of work surfaces. Dispensing with the traditional fixed links between media supplies and workplaces allows the free positioning of so-called

The design process

101

"media stations" which, in a similar way to individual machines, can be used wherever they are needed.

This dynamisation of the workplace creates space for better mounting and better use of the tools directly required, and with its avoidance of multiple connections at every station it also has a damping effect on costs. Questioning the traditional and sensibly reorganising a variety of interrelationships within the system have led to solutions which facilitate innovative structures and new aesthetics.

A multidisciplinary team was established to engineer and implement the system on the basis of the results obtained. Constant examination and control of all product characteristics such as ergonomics, functionality, ecology, system coherence, emotionality, formal quality and acceptance against the background of contemporary design led to the present product.

With the independence of the furnishings from the media supplies, maximum flexibility in handling the media is achieved. Compliance with a set dimensional grid results in a small number of elements with an extensive range of combinations. With the various system components, it is possible to construct both straight line laboratories of the traditional type for general use and to establish new, special laboratory structures for particular applications. There is an opportunity to use inserts and add-on elements to loosen up traditional structures and form niches, for instance where concentration is required on documentation work and suchlike. In the interplay with these more freely designed add-on components, the mc 6 system provides great freedom in functional and creative planning. Overlaps between different laboratory types require mixing of the various components at a single location. This is facilitated by the formal consistency of the basic elements and the formal relationships between the add-on parts, and leads to the creation and recreation of innovative and project-specific room situations with maximum flexibility. The demand for non-obsolescence is thus fulfilled to a great extent.

The system provides various media supply combinations. All the units can be supplied from the floor, from the ceiling, from the wall or from the new "media wing". This suspended structure with integrated lighting creates a new experience of the laboratory environment, and of the supporting technology.

1:1 prototype of the innovative media supply system

The design process

1st step: Study and initial approaches
- Actual status of laboratories and tradition
- Factors influencing the design framework
- Cultural influences
- The market
- Competing products
- Standards and regulations
- Structural analysis
- Ergonomics
- Future requirements

2nd step: Conceptual planning
- Structural considerations
- Morphology of the assemblies
- Initial sketches and representations
- Workflow study
- Ergonomic grid
- Material and colour concept
- Dimensional drawings
- Initial configuration examples
- System conditions
- Modular structure
- Testing with scale model
- First 1:1 mock-up
- Handling test

3rd step: Detailed planning
- Detailed design of the individual products
  (3 example products from the mc 6 modular system)
- Structural coordination
- Material selection and testing
- Sets of drawings for detail models
- Cost auditing
- Coordination of technical details
- Detailed mock-up on a 1:1 scale
- Construction of the first finished, functional prototype
- Planning examples
- Modularity testing

4th step: Implementation
- Coordination of detailed design
- Checking of details
- Coordination with suppliers and manufacturing
- Prototype inspection of the first components
- Detailed coordination
- Assistance for the market launch
- Further product support actions

New mc 6 room
structure (production)

A new workplace
configuration

The design process

Hin

Good advice can often be very expensive. Here, it is included in the price. For if you want to embark on the journey to success by design, you will of course need a few basic tips on how to protect your future investment in design – as is your right – from freeloaders, imitators and plagiarists.

Of course, it is also important to know what kind of costs one ought to expect for design. This is so difficult and at the same time so absolutely necessary in the design field because the market almost totally lacks transparency as to cost structures and cost volumes.

Over and above that, everyone who wants to devote more attention to design has to know which journals regularly provide the information needed.

Finally, it is also important to learn where and how businesses can win awards for their design efforts, receiving acclaim for the direction they have taken and communicating their success to the outside world.

All in all, design is a complex management function, which has to be approached both strategically and operationally. Design is an integral part of systematic quality management. This being so, the management of design issues is a special form of quality management which addresses all the relevant areas of the business in a lateral function in order to create and preserve certain values and standards. The aim is to achieve a value-orientated system of business management. To reach that aim, however, step by step, it is important to seek advice and internalise good recommendations.

In response to a journalist's question as to how much of the cost of a Mercedes Benz was attributable to design, Chief Designer Bruno Sacco replied, "exactly 75 DM". Asked how he knew that so precisely, he replied, "I know my budget". As a rule, it is not so easy to put a figure on the cost factor of design. And Bruno Sacco's calculation perhaps overlooked the fact that a Mercedes also contains a multitude of bought-in parts which represent a further design cost factor that cannot, however, be easily determined.

In a poll of companies by the Design Zentrum Nordrhein Westfalen in 1997, it became apparent that many businesses could not precisely calculate the cost factor of design because they regarded it as part of their development costs. There was no separate cost centre for design work. This is why only a very few companies have provided for design budgets in their annual planning. With the growing influence of design on corporate success in future, however, this situation could change soon in many organisations. But what criteria and cornerstone figures can such budget planning be based on?

Budgets and costings for design services from external designers working as contractors are not always easy to quantify, as there are no even remotely reliable rules offered by the market. Unlike architectural services, in Germany at least, the remuneration for design work is not governed by a mandatory scale of statutory fees, but is subject to the pros and contras of freely negotiable contracts. Companies which have not yet had any considerable experience in dealing with external designers often feel uncomfortable in this situation, as they have no points of reference. The quotations from two designers for one and the same job can, indeed, sometimes differ by more than 100 percent. This unregulated and opaque market situation brings considerable uncertainty into the business for both the clients and the designers, often even ending in litigation. The most important condition for cooperation is therefore the conclusion of a contract, drawn up as precisely as possible, with an attached specification or briefing, in which the services and consideration and the completion dates are set down in detail.

Fees for industrial design services
Design fees may vary greatly, depending on how well a designer or design studio is known and how much experience they have. The terms of payment may also take on a variety of forms. Design work is divided into various categories which reflect different requirements for creativity and expertise. The distinctions made are as a rule these:

1. Drafting and development work, including market and product analysis
Fee per hour: 100.00 DM to 300.00 DM

2. Finished artwork, CAD work, detail drawings etc.
Fee per hour: 60.00 DM to 100.00 DM

3. Model building
Fee per hour: 60.00 DM to 150.00 DM
Model building is also frequently subcontracted by design studios to third parties. In such cases, the costs incurred are generally passed on to the client.

4. Design consultancy
(project or company-related)
Fee per hour: 100.00 DM to 300.00 DM
and more

Licence fee
As designs are the intellectual property of their originators, design work is subject to an additional licence fee, which is not as a rule included in the fees listed above. A licence fee is only due when the client actually intends to manufacture and sell the product which has been designed. The only exception to this rule is the lump sum fee described below.

There are also various methods of calculating the licence fees, which are freely negotiable.

Lump sum fee
This remuneration is due once and for all on completion of the design work,

irrespective of whether the design is to be embodied in a product immediately, later or even not at all. On payment of the previously agreed lump sum, the rights to the design are transferred to the client. As a rule, however, further transfer of the rights to third parties is excluded. This means that only the client is entitled to use the design for his own purposes. He many not make the design available to another enterprise either for a fee or gratis, without the consent and possibly a further payment to the designer.

The amount of the lump sum fee is determined by the type of product and the estimation of its chances of being sold.

The fee can be between 4,000 DM and 50,000 DM, and even more.

Royalty from sales
In this case, royalties are paid for use of the design in proportion to the sales volume. The designer receives a percentage of the revenue for each product sold, based as a rule on the manufacturer's selling price to dealers. Here too, the amount of the royalty varies according to the type of product and the expected sales.

In some cases, when for example massive sales are expected, the entire design fee can be negotiated in the form of royalties. Then, the designer subjects his work fully to the entrepreneurial risk.

Royalties range between 1.0 percent and 5.0 percent of the manufacturer's selling price.

Fee based on results
This type of remuneration is only paid when a design is actually transformed into a product. If a company decides – for whatever reason – not to implement a design, the designer remains empty-handed. This does not however mean that all the design work was for nothing. That can be treated quite separately from this contingent licence fee. As the designer bears a greater risk when agreeing a fee based on results, this type of remuner ation is as a rule twice as high as a cor responding lump sum fee.

Fixed monthly sum
This method of payment is set down in a framework agreement covering a relatively long period, and provides for the payment of monthly, or indeed quarterly or six-monthly, lump sums. This system is however only to be recommended when there is a long-term working relationship between the manufacturer and designer, in which several products are developed and put on the market each year.

Fees for graphic design work
The fee situation for graphic design is somewhat different. In this field, companies can refer to recommended fee scales published by the two professional associations, the Federation of German Graphic Designers (BDG) and the Alliance of German Designers (AGD).

In many cases, manufacturers do not spend enough time finding out about the design studios they may wish to work with. The selection is frequently made on the basis of the cheapest quotation. That can however be more trouble and expense than it is worth, if the cheapest designer is the worst choice and knows little about the particular industry or product. A number of firms do not even stop at placing orders with design students, because they are prepared to work for a pittance. People who do that should really not have the cheek to complain if things do not go their way!

Find out first which design studios come into question as partners for your company. You can find this information in reference works like the annual international yearbooks on "Design Innovations" and "Communications Design", or in professional journals (see list in the appendix). In addition, you can request advice from your Chamber of Commerce or the Design Zentrum Nordrhein Westfalen. Remember: bad design is always more expensive than good design! Organise the collaboration with the design studio of your choice in a detailed contract. And before doing so, make sure you know what you want and what services you expect from the designer, and negotiate all terms of payment in advance.

Companies that back design and are successful in doing so very often find their successful products imitated by competitors. This is not only annoying, but also mostly leads to commercial disadvantages. But those who want to assert their intellectual property rights to the original product and embark upon litigation have no easy task in convincing the courts. That is above all almost impossible when they have neglected to apply for corresponding patent rights in good time.

In my work as an expert in design law matters I have very often found that being in the right and winning a court case are two different things. For it is a very rare event for a plagiarist slavishly to imitate a product. But even in a case like that, it can be difficult to assert one's rights if the manufacturer failed to apply for registration of the design of the original product.

Most plagiarists, however, imitate by aiming at the greatest possible similarity with the original product and only making changes in a few details or on the level of subordinate stylistic elements. Many judges react favourably to that, and refuse to accept that such cases are also illegal imitations.

Unfortunately, it is always possible to find designers who are prepared to create promising imitations. Serious companies will not, of course, stoop to utilising their services.

There is no "design law" as such in Germany. Nevertheless, it is possible to obtain legally effective protection for newly developed products. The ideal thing is to design a product which is so original and formally unique as a work of art. This certainly demands an unusual degree of creative power in product design. In such a case, the product would be covered by copyright law and thus enjoy the best possible protection against imitators. The courts, though, are only prepared to acknowledge copyright in design in very few cases. For this reason, the only remedy available in a dispute is as a rule the assertion of a registered design. This is however absolutely dependent on the timely application for a registered design for that new product from the German Patent Office in Berlin. Otherwise, the chances of success are very slim.

One thing is clear: it is by no means easy to assert one's rights successfully in matters of design law. Just how complicated it is to find out which field of law may provide a remedy becomes clear when one considers how many different possibilities there are.

The Hamburg-based lawyer Christian Klawitter once described the problem complex of design and law as follows: "Design law is not a legal term, but rather the empirical designation for a field of jurisprudence that extends over several laws, these being essentially the law of registered designs, copyright law and competition law. All these laws dovetail together, supplementing or mutually excluding each other."

Conclusion

Without a registered design there is little prospect of success in pursuing claims against plagiarists. For not every imitation of other people's products is prohibited! If no intellectual or industrial property rights are there to oppose the plagiarist, the imitation is as a rule permissible, unless it can be proved to constitute unfair competition.

Companies often want to wait and see whether a new product is actually successful before applying for a registered design. But then it may already be too late! For a product can only be reliably protected when it is new and original at the time of registration. When a product has been on the market for some time without a registration, however, it is no longer new, as it has achieved a certain degree of familiarity simply by being there. In this way, the successful and therefore well known product disqualifies itself from subsequent classification as an innovation. That's how complex legislation can be.

An application for a registered design to protect a product should be submitted in good time before the market launch to the Deutsches Patentamt, Dienststelle Berlin, Gitschiner Strasse 97, 10969 Berlin.

It is essential to ensure that the characteristic and unique design features are described in full. They should be documented as accurately as possible and clearly illustrated in photographs.

For in the case of a dispute, the court will not compare the products concerned, but rather the deposited photographs of product A with those of product B. Even minor deviations between the registered sample and the later series product can lead to loss of the registered design. An experienced lawyer with the relevant specialisation should therefore always be consulted.

Germany has more design competitions than any other country. Design prizes are awarded in almost all of the individual states. Further information can be obtained from the various design centres, chambers of commerce and industry, or the ministries of economic affairs.

Entering design competitions is another way of enhancing the status of a product. Design awards are an additional sales argument, and increase the acceptance of a product on the market.

The German awards with international significance include the following:

The Red Dot
for High and the Highest Design Quality
Design Innovations Competition
Awarded annually

Design Zentrum Nordrhein Westfalen
Gelsenkirchener Strasse 181
D-45309 Essen

if
Industrie Forum Design Hannover
Awarded annually

Industrie Forum Design Hannover
Messegelände
D-30521 Hannover

Federal Prize for Product Design
Only open to products which have already received an award in another competition.
Awarded every 2 years

Contact:
German Design Council / Rat für Formgebung
P.O. Box 15 03 11
D-60327 Frankfurt am Main

German Prize for Communications Design
The first prize is worth 20,000 DM.
Awarded annually

Design Zentrum Nordrhein Westfalen
Gelsenkirchener Strasse 181
D-45309 Essen

Success by design presupposes constant familiarity with the latest developments and trends in design. There are numerous magazines in Germany dealing more or less specifically with current design events.

The most important design journals are listed below. Apologies are offered for any omissions, but in the space available it would be impossible to present an exhaustive list.

German language design magazines

arcade
Fachzeitschrift für Möbel, Leuchten, Objekte
Adress
Ferdinand Holzmann Verlag GmbH
Mexikoring 37
D-22297 Hamburg
Tel.: +49–40–6 32 01 80
Fax: +49–40–6 30 75 10
Issues: 6 per year

design report
Publisher
German Design Councl, Frankfurt am Main
Adress
Blue C. Verlag, stilwerk
Große Elbstraße 68
D-22767 Hamburg
Tel.: +49–40–30 6 21 400
Fax: +49–40–30 6 21 409
E-mail: designreport@macup.com
Internet: www.euro-design-guide.de/design-report
Issues: 10 per year

design report is a magazine addressed to a wide audience and follows current events very closely. The individual issues report in an entertaining fashion on selected focal topics.

design report is recommended as a good accompaniment to form magazine.

form
Zeitschrift für Gestaltung
Founded by Jupp Ernst,
Wilhelm Sandberg, Curt Schweicher and Wilhelm Wagenfeld
Publishers
Alex Buck and Karlheinz Krug
Adress
Hanauer Landstraße 161
D-60314 Frankfurt am Main
Tel.: +49–69–94 33 25 0
Fax: +49–69–94 33 25 25
E-mail: form@form de
Internet: www.form.de
Issues: 6 per year

md
moebel interior design
Publishers
Konrad Kohlhammer, Prof. Dieter Zimmer
Editor in chief: Ulrich Büttner
Adress
Conradin Verlag
Robert Kohlhammer GmbH
Ernst-Mey-Straße 8
D-70771 Leinfelden-Echterdingen
Tel.: +49-7 11-75 94 0
Fax: +49-7 11-75 94 390
Issues: monthly

MENSCH & BÜRO
Editor in chief: Hans Ottomann
Adress
Mensch & Büro Verlags GmbH
Neckarstraße 121
D-70190 Stuttgart
Tel.: +49-7 11-2 63 10
Fax: +49-7 11-2 63 12 92
E-mail: red.mub@t-online.de
Internet: www.menschundbuero.de
Issues: 6 per year

novum gebrauchsgrafik
Das Forum für Kommunikations-Design
Publisher
Erhardt D. Stiebner, Dr. Jörg D. Stiebner
Editors: Brigitta Nitsch (verantw.),
Uwe Richter, Bettina Ulrich, Gabriela von
Wachter
Adress
F. Bruckmann München Verlag +
Druck GmbH & Co. Produkt KG
Nymphenburger Straße 86
D-80636 München
Tel.: +49-89-1 25 73 22
Fax: +49-89-1 25 73 18
Issues: monthly

OFFICE DESIGN
Das Magazin für Business und Design
Editor in chief
W. O. Geberzahn
Adress
Mörikestraße 16
D-73525 Schwäbisch Gmünd
Tel.: +49-71 71-92 91 24
Fax: +49-71 71-92 91 25
E-mail: Geberzahn@T-online.de
Issues: quarterly

Office Design magazine is now in its 14th year, and the focus of its reporting has shifted in recent years towards business-related topics. The issues deal with a selected current topic and events in the fields of architecture, marketing, new work, offices and corporate identity. It is a useful guide to subjects which involve but also go beyond the bounds of design per se.

PAGE
Das Computermagazin für Kreative
Adress
MACup Verlag GmbH
Leverkusenstraße 54
D-22761 Hamburg
Tel.: +49-40-85 18 33 50
Fax: +49-40-85 18 34 49

The following magazine was launched in June 1999:

red dot
Magazin des Design Zentrums
Nordrhein Westfalen
Editor: Dagmar Ostermann
Adress
c/o Design Zentrum Nordrhein Westfalen
Gelsenkirchener Straße 181
D-45309 Essen
Tel.: +49–2 01–30 10 4–19
Fax: +49–2 01–30 10 4–40
E-mail:
design_germany@compuserve.com
Issues: 1 per year

forum design magazine is aimed at entrepreneurs and senior and middle managers. The topics are intended to increase the awareness of design among managers with decision-making authority.

International design magazines

Abitare
Editrice Abitare Segesta S.p.A.
Corso Monforte 15
I-20122 Milano

AXIS
World Design Journal
5-17-1 Roppongi, Minato-Ku
J-Tokyo, 106

Blueprint
Wordsearch Ltd.
Christ Church Cosway Street
GB-London NW1 5NJ

Domus
Editorial Domus
Via Achille Graudi 5/7
I-20089 Rozzano (Milano)

Hochparterre
Illustrierte für Gestaltung und Architektur
Ausstellungstraße 25
CH-8004 Zürich

I.D.
International Design Magazine
440 Park Avenue South, 14th Floor
USA-New York, NY 10016

Modo
Design Magazine
R.O.E. Ricerche Design
Editrice Sri
Via Roma 21
I-20094 Corsico (Milano)

Nikkei Design
Nikkei Business Publications, Inc.
1-1 Ogawamachi, kanda Chiyoda-ku
J-Tokyo, 101

Hints + tips

Acknowledgements

My special thanks are due to all those companies without whose support and provision of information, materials and photos, this book would not have been possible. They are the following:

AUTHENTICS
artipresent GmbH
Max-Eyth-Straße 30
71088 Holzgerlingen
Tel.: 0 70 31–68 05 0
Fax: 0 70 31–68 05 99

Hansgrohe
Postfach 11 45
77757 Schiltach
Tel.: 0 78 36–51 0
Fax: 0 78 36–51 13 00

basta.
Innovation & Design GmbH
Jungstraße 14
42277 Wuppertal
Tel.: 0202–50 19 42
Fax: 0202–50 02 91

BMW AG
Postfach
80788 Munich
Tel.: 0 89–38 24 54 48
Fax: 0 89–38 24 36 96

Braun AG
Frankfurter Straße 145
61476 Kronberg/Taunus
Tel.: 0 61 73–30 26 30
Fax: 0 61 73–30 27 27

Daimler-Benz AG
Epplestraße 225
70567 Stuttgart
Tel.: 07 11–17 9 68 64
Fax: 07 11–17 9 82 47

Duravit AG
Postfach 240
78128 Hornberg
Tel.: 0 78 33–70 0
Fax: 0 78 33–70 289

Festo AG & Co.
Ruiter Straße 82
73734 Esslingen
Tel.: 07 11–347 38 50
Fax: 07 11–347 38 99

Ford Werke AG
Henry-Ford-Straße 2
50735 Cologne
Tel.: 02 21–90 0
Fax: 02 21–90 1 26 41

FSB Franz Schneider Brakel
GmbH + Co
Nieheimer Straße 38
33034 Brakel
Tel.: 0 52 72–6 08 0
Fax: 0 52 72–6 08 300

Verlag form GmbH
Hanauer Landstarße 161
60314 Frankfurt am Main
Tel.: 0 69–94 33 25 0
Fax: 0 69–94 33 25 25

Hoesch Metall +
Kunststoffwerk GmbH & Co.
Postfach 10 04 24
52304 Düren
Tel.: 0 24 22–54 0
Fax: 0 24 22–67 93

IBM Deutschland
Informationssysteme GmbH
Pascalstraße 100
70569 Stuttgart
Tel.: 0 70 31–16 66 13
Fax: 0 70 31–16 69 07

Küppersbusch AG
Küppersbuschstraße 16
45883 Gelsenkirchen
Tel.: 02 09–4 01 0
Fax: 02 09–4 01 303

C. Josef Lamy GmbH
Grenzhöfer Weg 32
69123 Heidelberg
Tel.: 0 62 21–8 43 0
Fax: 0 62 21–8 43 132

Burkhardt Leitner constructiv
Am Bismarckturm 39
70192 Stuttgart
Tel.: 07 11–2 55 88 0
Fax: 07 11–2 55 88 11

Loewe Opta GmbH
Industriestraße 11
96317 Kronach
Tel.: 0 92 61–99 0
Fax: 0 92 61–95 411

M & M Uhren GmbH
Schiess-Straße 72
40549 Düsseldorf
Tel.: 02 11–53 74 01 0
Fax: 02 11–53 74 01 99

Herman Miller Limited
Niederlassung Deutschland
Kaiserswerther Straße 85
40878 Ratingen
Tel.: 0 21 02–74 288 0
Fax: 0 21 02–74 288 80

moll design
Reiner Moll & Partner
Turmgasse 7
73525 Schwäbisch Gmünd
Tel.: 0 71 71–93 00 0
Fax: 0 71 71–93 00 23

Nissan Motor
Deutschland GmbH
Nissan Platz 1
41468 Neuss
Tel.: 0 21 31–3 88 430
Fax: 0 21 31–3 55 99

Verlagsgruppe
Handelsblatt GmbH
Office Design
Kasernenstraße 67
40213 Düsseldorf
Tel.: 02 11–88 7 0
Fax: 02 11–88 7 14 10

C. Hugo Pott GmbH
Ritterstraße 28
42659 Solingen
Tel.: 02 12–4 30 56
Fax: 02 12–4 24 25

Recaro GmbH & Co.
Stuttgarter Straße 73
73230 Kirchheim/Teck
Tel.: 0 70 21–93 5 187
Fax: 0 70 21–93 5 339

Deutsche Renault AG
Kölner Weg 6-10
50321 Brühl
Tel.: 0 22 32–73 270
Fax: 0 22 32–73 395

Optische Werke G. Rodenstock
Isartalstraße 43
80469 Munich
Tel.: 0 89–72 02 745
Fax: 0 89–72 02 749

Peter Schmidt Studios
Feldbrunnenstraße 27
20148 Hamburg
Tel.: 0 40–44 18 04 0
Fax: 0 40–44 18 04 70

Sieger Design
Schloß Harkotten
48336 Sassenberg
Tel.: 0 54 26–94 92 18
Fax: 0 54 26–38 75

Simon & Goetz
Darmstädter Landstraße 180
60598 Frankfurt am Main
Tel.: 0 69–96 88 55 0
Fax: 0 69–96 88 55 23

Sony Deutschland GmbH
Hugo-Eckener-Straße 20
50829 Cologne
Tel.: 02 21–59 66 0
Fax: 02 21–59 66 349

Tupperware Deutschland GmbH
Praunheimer Landstraße 70
60488 Frankfurt am Main
Tel.: 0 69–7 68 02 0
Fax: 0 69–7 68 02 299

Vitra GmbH
Charles-Eames-Straße 2
79576 Weil am Rhein
Tel.: 0 76 21–70 23 328
Fax: 0 76 21–70 24 30

Wilkhahn
Wilkening + Hahne GmbH + Co.
Postfach 20 35
31844 Bad Münder
Tel.: 0 50 42–999 0
Fax: 0 50 42–999 226

WMF Württembergische
Metallwarenfabrik AG
Eberhardstraße
73309 Geislingen/Steige
Tel.: 0 73 31–25 1
Fax: 0 73 31–4 53 87

Bibliography

Otl Aicher:
Analog und digital;
Berlin 1991

Otl Aicher:
Die Welt als Entwurf;
Berlin 1991

Otl Aicher:
Typographie;
Berlin 1992

Gustav Bergmann:
Umweltgerechtes Produkt-
Design; Management und
Marketing zwischen Ökonomie
und Ökologie;
Neuwied/Kriftel/Berlin 1994

Bernhard E. Bürdek:
Design; Geschichte, Theorie
und Praxis der Produkt-
gestaltung;
Cologne 1991

Rido Busse:
Was kostet Design?;
Kostenkalkulation für Designer
und ihre Auftraggeber;
Frankfurt am Main 1998

Gillo Dorfles:
Gute Industrieform und ihre
Ästhetik;
Munich 1964

Norbert Hammer (Ed.):
Die stillen Designer – Manager
des Designs;
Essen 1994

Thomas Hauffe:
Design Schnellkurs;
Cologne 1995

Wolfgang Kinnebrock:
Marketing mit Multimedia; Neue
Wege zum Kunden;
Landsberg/Lech 1994

Udo Koppelmann:
Produktmarketing; Entschei-
dungsgrundlage für Produkt-
manager;
Berlin (Springer-Verlag) 1993

Raymond Loewy:
Häßlichkeit verkauft sich
schlecht;
Düsseldorf 1953

Christian Marquart:
Industriekultur – Industriedesign;
Ein Stück deutscher Wirtschafts-
und Designgeschichte;
Berlin (undated)

Donald Normann:
Die Dinge des Alltags;
Frankfurt am Main/New York
1989

Rat für Formgebung (Ed.):
Design-Management;
Düsseldorf/Wien/New York
(ECON) 1990

Rat für Formgebung (Ed.):
Klaus Jürgen Maack;
Design oder die Kultur des
Angemessenen;
Frankfurt am Main (undated)

Carlo Rummel:
Designmanagement;
Wiesbaden 1995

Klaus Schmidt (Ed.):
Corporate Identity in Europa;
Strategien, Instrumente,
Erfolgreiche Beispiele;
Frankfurt am Main/New York
1994

Claudius A. Schmitz (Ed.):
Managementfaktor Design;
Munich 1994

Gert Selle:
Geschichte des Design in
Deutschland;
Frankfurt am Main/New York
1994

Armin Töpfer/Hartmut
Mehdorn:
Total Quality Management;
Anforderungen und Umsetzung
im Unternehmen;
Neuwied/Kriftel/Berlin 1994

Kurt Weidemann:
Wo der Buchstabe das Wort
führt; Ansichten über Schrift
und Typographie;
Bonn 1997

Hans Wichmann (Ed.):
System-Design. Bahnbrecher;
Hans Gugelot 1920-1965;
Munich 1984

Jens Wonigeit:
Total Quality Management;
Grundzüge und Effizienz-
analyse;
Wiesbaden 1994

Peter Zec:
Design goes virtual; Entwürfe
zur Ästhetik in der
Informationsgesellschaft;
Essen 1996

Peter Zec (Ed.):
Design Innovations Yearbook '97
Essen 1997

Peter Zec (Ed.):
Design Innovations Yearbook '98
Essen 1998

Peter Zec:
german design standards;
Cologne 1997

Peter Zec (Ed.):
Handbuch für Multimediadesign,
Industriedesign, Fotodesign,
Kommunikationsdesign in
Nordrhein-Westfalen 1996/97;
Essen 1996

Peter Zec (Ed.):
Handbuch für Industriedesign,
Fotodesign, Kommunikations-
design in Nordrhein-Westfalen
1993/94;
Essen 1993

Peter Zec:
Informationsdesign;
Die organisierte Kommunikation;
Osnabrück 1988

Peter Zec (Ed.):
Internationales Jahrbuch
Kommunikations-Design
1996/97;
Frankfurt am Main 1996

Peter Zec (Ed.):
Internationales Jahrbuch
Kommunikations-Design
1997/98;
Frankfurt am Main 1997

Peter Zec (Ed.):
LebensForm Tupperware – Die
Kultivierung des Gebrauchs;
Essen 1997

Peter Zec und Vito Orazem (Ed.):
Über den Herd – Eine kleine
Kultur- und Designgeschichte
der Kochstelle;
Essen 1995

Eugen Zeitherer:
Industrie-Design; Entwicklung –
Produktion – Ökonomie;
Stuttgart 1991

Photographs

Andreas Fechner Visuelle
Kommunikation, Wesel
Page 2

AKG Berlin photo, Berlin
Page 14

Frank Schuberth, Essen
Pages 16, 17 and 73

Mario Pignata-Monti
Page 33

Markus Richter, Stuttgart
Page 33

Hans Hansen, Hamburg
Pages 45, 47, 49 and 50

Christian Coigny
Page 51

Richard Bryant
Page 51

Works photos, Design Zentrum
Nordrhein Westfalen archives
Pages 12, 13, 14, 15, 16, 17, 20,
21, 22, 23, 24, 25, 26, 28, 29, 30,
31, 34, 40, 41, 42, 51, 53, 54, 55,
59, 60, 61, 62, 64, 65, 66, 67, 68,
69, 70, 71, 77, 78, 79, 80, 81, 82,
83, 84, 86, 87, 88, 89, 92, 93, 94,
95, 96, 100, 101, 102, 103, 113,
114 and 115